WHEN NOT PERFORMING

For Steve —
Thanks for your interest!
All the Best
[signature]

WHEN NOT PERFORMING

New Orleans Musicians

[signature]

Photography by
David G. SPIELMAN

Text by
Fred LYON

PELICAN PUBLISHING COMPANY

Gretna 2012

The word "Pelican" and the depiction of a pelican are
trademarks of Pelican Publishing Company, Inc., and are
registered in the U.S. Patent and Trademark Office.

Library of Congress Cataloging-in-Publication Data

Spielman, David G., 1950-
  When not performing / photography by David G. Spielman ; text by Fred Lyon.
    p. cm.
  ISBN 978-1-4556-1756-2 (hardcover : alk. paper) -- ISBN 978-1-4556-1757-9 (e-book) 1. Musicians--Louisiana--New Orleans--Portraits. I. Lyon, Fred. II. Title.
  ML87.S626 2012
  780.92'276335--dc23

                                                              2012021003

Printed in China
Published by Pelican Publishing Company, Inc.
1000 Burmaster Street, Gretna, Louisiana 70053

CONTENTS

PREFACE

Musicians and photographers are similar in many respects. A musician will play whether or not he or she is getting paid. The music, whether from a piano, guitar, horn, or banjo, has to be expelled from the body, out from the heart and soul and into the open air. Photographers—true photographers—will go out shooting whenever time permits. There need not be an assignment. Different weather, something or someone new—just being able to shoot and the possibility of capturing that exceptional shot is what a photographer lives for. In the same way, musicians will perform for the sheer pleasure of being able to play. The music, their music, is in them and it has to be released. Some of their greatest successes happen when, through their own self-expression, they make a clear and profound statement. I'm not suggesting that musicians and photographers not get paid in order to fuel their artistic genius. Instead, what is being said is that most artists, whether they be musicians, writers, or painters, will continue to work, tune, and fine-tune their craft and talents regardless of whether any money is involved. In acknowledging that simple fact, we are all the benefactors of their devotion to their art.

A project like this one didn't come about in a flash. The project started long before the first photo was ever taken. As with musicians, writers, and other creative types, seeds and kernels are gathered along life's way. Events and occurrences happen during a lifetime that then will set the course. My course began as a little boy, hearing my father tell me that "Louis Armstrong's name and music was recognized all around the world." Hearing and seeing the power and poise that musicians controlled had a thunderous effect. Growing up under the influences of Elvis, Bob Dylan, the Beatles, Dizzy Gillespie, and Miles Davis, and then spending my senior year of college in Vienna and being exposed to Bach, Brahms, and Strauss, the seeds and kernels were planted for this project.

Throughout my formal education and evolution as a photographer, I studied the history and mastery of Walker Evans, Edward Weston, Ansel Adams, Arnold Newman, André Kertész, Alfred Eisenstaedt, Gordon Parks, Brassaï, and Henri Cartier-Bresson and came to realize that I wanted to shoot places, spaces, and faces. I wanted to tell stories with my images. My goal was to travel, see, learn, and photograph as much as possible.

Enter New Orleans, 1973. Having never been here but thinking it was the most exotic, European city in the U.S., I was going to launch my life as a photographer. My Oklahoma upbringing and my European education did not prepare me for what I was about to find and discover. Meat and potatoes gave way to raw oysters and pinching and peeling crawfish. The sights, sounds, and smells washed over me with a life-changing effect. It was everywhere, all the time—clubs, concerts, and street parades were a common occurrence. Tyler's Beer Garden, the Maple Leaf Bar, Rosy's Jazz Hall, Tipitina's, and the Warehouse were all part of my crash course to the city, New Orleans 101. Then came more than just places, but personalities and talents as well: Pete Fountain,

Dr. John, Al Hirt, the Nevilles, Allen Toussaint, Dave Bartholomew, Fats Domino, and Frogman Henry recreated all that I knew about music. It seemed that wherever I turned, seeds and kernels kept sprouting.

As a young, struggling photographer just starting out, I wanted to decipher and photograph New Orleans but needed a plan. Partying and living the nightlife would have been easy, but my work and dreams would have suffered. Moderation had to be enforced, and all of these tidbits had to be saved, filed, and put away. Knowing that I couldn't rush into a project and that I didn't know enough, I had to continue to observe, gather information, keep field notes, and mature as a person and as a photographer. Slowly, I started to find my way to the photographic works of Clarence Laughlin, Michael A. Smith, Gordon Parks, and Walker Evans. Their images provided me with lots of information on how the South lived and honored its past. Ingesting their work and words, I was becoming a student of this cultural oasis that was right outside my front door, around the corner, or down an alley from wherever I was standing or staying at any given time. Then the works of Ralston Crawford and Lee Friedlander introduced me to the musical icons of their periods. During that segregated time, they documented and introduced the world to New Orleans Jazz. Now, all I had to do was figure out how to capture it. I didn't want to rush forward without gaining the respect and trust of the musicians. I wanted to earn both their respect and their friendship. All the while, I wanted to find my visual voice and make the images

my own. For a subject such as New Orleans music and its musicians, that was going to prove to be challenging. How do you photograph the same subject yet capture it with a different view?

Little by little, ever so slowly, I was introduced to and got to photograph some of the greats: Pete Fountain, Al Hirt, Willie and Percy Humphrey, Doc Cheatham, Danny Barker, and others. Talking with and being invited into their homes, I began to see and understand that their lives weren't all that much different from ours. The only difference was clear: they were possessed and driven by their music, not in an unhealthy way, but by something in their marrow that required—demanded—them to play and perform. Being told of and invited to several Jazz Funerals (those of Tommy Rigley, Jim Robinson, and Danny Barker), I came to realize and understand how this musical mosaic is a continuous work in progress. These men and women were and are part of something bigger than themselves, their group, or their song. With great respect and reverence for those who came before, they would come and perform to honor the passing of one of their own. Upon the death of Wardell Quezergue, Dr. John said that each one of these deaths and funerals represented the closing of another chapter in the musical history of New Orleans.

Clearly, music is vital to their lives and to the life of the city. With that knowledge, interest, and admiration, I was determined to photograph them and try to convey their stories. The musicians themselves are strikingly different. Their life stories have been filled with the entire spectrum of trials and tribulations. Their experiences challenge the characters of some of the greatest southern novels. Poverty, abuse, drugs, fame, exploitation, love, and loss are all part of the pedigree that gives them the soul, torment, passion, and raw talent. At the same time, their stories are our stories. Their sounds and words guide and soothe us in our moments of joy and grief. Several of the subjects have suffered from different addictions, some have spent time in jail, but in all cases, when they were released or when they beat back their demons, they all returned to their music and their instruments. Most, when asked where they wanted to be photographed, had great and meaningful ideas. A very large percentage wanted to be photographed with their instrument at their side. Clearly, that instrument is an extension of their being, their soul mate and partner and not unlike what my camera is to me. Always at my side, always ready to take another picture—I am defined by my images just as they are defined by their music. They are musicians, plain and simple. Without their instruments, they are people just like you and me.

Another question that I had to face in preparing myself for this project was to consider how it is that New Orleans still remains the cog in the musical wheel. We all know the history of why most of it started and how it grew. The slave trade, the Mississippi River, and the proximity to the Caribbean Islands all contributed greatly and dearly to this musical heartland. New Orleans has been battered and beaten through the years, not only by storms but also by economics and recessions. And yet, every time, the music and its students and fans return. Culture can't be cultivated in a classroom or taught in a workshop, it is a major component of our molecular make-up. We don't just go and listen to it in a club or concert hall, it wafts from our windows, our schools, and our cars. It surrounds us as much as the humidity does. It pours from our pores, it lingers on our breath, whether we play or don't play. Most often it is passed down the family line from parents to sons and daughters, but sometimes it travels from house to house and neighbor to neighbor. Women and men alike, from all over this country and around the world, travel here to live in and absorb it. Many come, but not so many leave. Once bitten, it is almost impossible to get New Orleans out of your bloodstream, head, and heart.

As an observer and as a photographer, I felt the time was right for this project. My education was coming to an end. The musicians and photographic mentors, alive and dead, had spoken clearly and forcefully. I hope I've earned my chops. Had I tried this in my youth, it probably would have been loud and proud, missing the subtleties and nuances that make the music universal and yet unique to the individual all at the same time. With age and experience, I've heard and seen much more. Music is a language for your ears, photography for your eyes. In an interview, Joe Walsh said, "A philosopher once said as we live life, it looks like random anarchy, one event smashing into another. But when you look back, life looks like a finely crafted novel." This book is an uncompleted puzzle. Pieces and parts are still missing, not because Fred and I couldn't find them but because there are far too many. The border and boundaries of this puzzle haven't been defined, because new pieces are forming and being made all the time. The challenge to you as a reader is to look at our pieces, find your own, and complete your own puzzle. New influences find their way here with every plane that arrives, every ship that anchors, and every car that drives and parks in the Quarter. Our culture isn't hard and fast. It is a large sponge that will absorb any and all who get close enough.

In my years here, I have absorbed most of what New Orleans has to offer: its art, architecture, literature, food, and (of course) music. Many still consider me an interloper, someone not really from here, and I am often viewed with a weary eye. Not being able to claim a local high school or a hospital where I was born, I will always be an outsider to some. Having stayed through Katrina and published a book of photographs about southern writers, many are still skeptical. The famous photographer Ansel Adams said, "The negative is the equivalent of the composer's score and the print the performance." I'm hoping my "performance" will put to rest any skepticism and trepidation that may still be lurking about. For a very old city, we continue to be and act very young. As in photography, painting, writing, and all other art forms, one must study the past in order to challenge and make the future. History is a great and wonderful teacher, but the main lesson should be to not be afraid to push and bump up against the status quo, stretching and pushing the boundaries as we go. Louis Armstrong said, "My whole life, my whole soul, my whole spirit is to blow that horn . . ." His words express clearly how I feel about my photography.

The seeds and kernels, sown so long ago, have been nurtured and harvested. I sincerely hope you enjoy them.

David G. Spielman
New Orleans

ACKNOWLEDGMENTS

DAVID G. SPIELMAN

A project such as this involves so many people that it's hard to know where to start and how to stop. I am forever grateful to the musicians who so freely gave of their time and knowledge to help (and ultimately become) this project. For without them, whom would I shoot?

Fred Lyon, the writer of the text, was such an important part of the process. His research and writing rounds out the images, giving a fuller and richer view of the people captured.

The photographic process is a lesson in organization, negatives, scans, and test prints, and the juggling of dates and schedules is the critical ingredient that makes it all fit. If something is misplaced, lost, or misfiled, it becomes the proverbial needle in the haystack. Britt Melancon was there, helping me keep it all straight and moving forward. His darkroom and digital skills added greatly to my finished product.

The inspiration comes from other photographers: Lee Friedlander, Walker Evans, Margaret Bourke-White, Henri Cartier-Bresson, Bruce Davidson, and Gordon Parks, whose work inspires, challenges, and drives me to do my best. I am also indebted to Clarence Giese, a painter, the friend who in the 1970s in Vienna taught me to look, so I could see the images that I wanted and needed to take.

This is for Shelley and Sasha, my wife and son, who make me whole and exceedingly happy.

FRED LYON

I am deeply grateful to my extraordinary wife, Lynn, my creative muse and passionate partner in pursuing the many pleasures of New Orleans; to my children, whose patience and support through all of the times when "Pop is working on the book again" abounded; to my friend and talented collaborator, David Spielman, for letting me ride shotgun while we explored the streets of New Orleans on what proved to be an amazing journey; to my friend Sonny Shields, who in the 1970s taught me what it meant to love New Orleans; to his wife, Laura, whose gracious hospitality defines the city in which her family has lived since the 1850s; and, finally, to the people and the city of New Orleans, which often engage, occasionally infuriate, and always inspire.

PHOTOGRAPHER'S NOTES

Here in New Orleans, music is a fabric woven into our everyday lives; it is everywhere, all the time. We watch our musicians grow up, grow old, and even die. They teach the young and leave a legacy behind for all of us. They are part of our extended families, entertaining us at sweet-sixteen parties, high school graduations, engagements, weddings, bar mitzvahs, festivals, block parties, and more. They live among us as family members and neighbors and share our good times, our food, our culture, and our love.

For years, I have photographed them at many different events and venues, always leaving the scene feeling as if there was so much more to them than their stage life. The late Michael P. Smith covered the concert and club scene from the late sixties until his death. His photographic body of work stands alone as a tribute to his dedication and devotion to the music and the musicians. He shot the first Jazz Fest and the thirty-four years after that. His body of work is unique. When I arrived in New Orleans, he was well established and I didn't think I would or could do a better job than he. I needed to do something different. I needed to find my visual voice of how to tell the musician's story. Another image of them performing wasn't enough for me and my photography. I wanted to know more about what they do when they aren't on stage, so I started getting to know them while not performing.

My interests have always leaned toward the creative processes of the artists. I enjoy looking behind the curtain, so to speak, and seeing what makes them click. Why do people write, paint, cook, or play music? Most cannot make a great living from it: long nights, road trips, fast food, cheap hotels—but yet, the dream is there, very much alive in each and every one of them, always looking for the great audience, waiting for the perfect song, playing the coolest gig, or composing the sonic masterpiece. We are the luckier for their dream and their continuing passion to make and produce it!

Fred Lyon, who has written the text for this book, is a friend of mine. One night, while talking at a wedding reception, we discussed the depth and caliber of music in and of New Orleans. He asked me why I hadn't done a photographic book on musicians. I told him that I wanted to, but I hadn't found the right writer who matched my curiosity of a behind-the-scenes look. The one thing I knew for sure was that it would not be of them performing. These were going to be personal and private portraits, something similar to another book I had done years before, *Southern Writers,* in which I photographed authors in their workspaces. No glamour shots or over-produced glossies, but black and white portraits of them having just finished or getting ready to work. It was a treasured peek into how and why they wrote. Was it with a pencil, typewriter, or computer? Did they stand or sit, work late into the night or rise early? What was it that made them tick?

That conversation at the wedding was where this project all started. Where to begin? How to begin? We started compiling lists of musicians, types of music, and people to whom we needed to speak to give us insight to the musical community. In the end, it was the musicians themselves who helped provide many of the introductions. Once we started contacting musicians and they understood our direction, they were all in. Each of them chose his or her own location for the shoot. In many cases, it was where they played their first gig, their childhood home, or where they found their muse—a porch, garden, kitchen, alleyway, or club entrance. It was their choice, as it spoke to them in some way and gave us that glimpse of a life rarely seen by most.

We knew we couldn't produce the anthology of New Orleans music, as the book would have to be a tome. Plus, the music and its musicians are like our food: always changing. So our goal was to provide a window to look through, showing the tone, tenor, and diversity of what New Orleans has to offer and helping to educate and stimulate interest in one of our greatest assets.

Tracking down musicians isn't easy. Many are like smoke, easy to see but hard to capture. Ever-changing schedules, late nights, frequent road trips all add to the difficult task of finding and scheduling them. Even when that had been accomplished, musicians can be and are forgetful. Herding cats or trying to pick up mercury might have been easier. Time doesn't seem to be a high priority. There were several no-shows. However, when contact was made and the appointments were met, everything became magical. Each was a treasure of personality and stories. Their musical life was usually a unique road map of experiences, with people helping or mentoring them at just the right time, reinforcing the adage that music is the universal language. Stumbling blocks littered their travel; vices and devices helped and hindered their development. Yet time and time again, they found their way back to their music and home.

The project took on the qualities of a map of hidden treasure, a scavenger hunt of sorts, always revealing yet another gem that New Orleans has to offer of a neighborhood diner, café, or joint compiled from the body of their stories. Their tales told of how the musical bloodlines run. It was an educational experience unto itself, a crash course of the genealogy of New Orleans.

Working quickly, not wanting to disrupt their lives or schedules, I shot with available light and with very little equipment. Supplemental lighting was only used to complement what was there. There was no propping or rearranging furniture. I always shoot it as I find it; I want the viewers to see it as it is. My theory is that the more gear and the more people added to the mix, the more the photographer gets steered away from the proposed goal of getting into the personal space and personality of the subject. This is truly the epitome of less is more. I'm not interested in seeing the performer. I want to see, know, and photograph the person. Doc Cheatham, the trumpeter, once said, "If you want them to hear, play loud. If you want them to listen, play soft." That is how I approach my photography. With all my personal work, I shoot with Leica rangefinder cameras—small, quiet, non-threatening pieces of the finest photographic equipment made. No motor drives, no zoom lenses, just me, my Leica and the subject! Shooting this project was a great experience and as fascinating as it was fun. My hope is that you will enjoy the photographs as much as I enjoyed capturing them. All the best!

WRITER'S NOTES

My friend David Spielman has aptly described the genesis of this book: the magic and inspiration of the city's musicians, the process of the book's creation, and the challenges it has provided. More than most other places, New Orleans defines itself through its musicians, and these musicians in turn define themselves through the special city in which they live. It is, in some ways, a closed loop—the musicians need New Orleans, and New Orleans needs the musicians. By capturing these artists when not performing, in places of their own choosing, we are attempting to show the symbiotic relationship between the performers and the city they call home.

The conversations with each artist were relaxed, not a formal interview. There were no preconceived questions, and the musicians directed the conversation. We followed along, delighted to be allowed a glimpse behind what David describes as the "creative curtain." While we wanted to know why New Orleans is such a special place for music, it was not a question we typically had to ask.

Their answers inevitably emerged as they talked about the city's clubs, its jazz funerals and second line parades, its inter-connected families and neighborhoods, its churches, its festivals, its high school marching bands—all the elements combine to make New Orleans one of the rich musical incubators of the world.

Hurricane Katrina convinced me to move to New Orleans. In order to help preserve what was almost lost—its music, its legends—I needed to have my feet planted firmly on the city's scarred and sacred ground. I found that whatever damage had been done on the surface, the roots of the city's music were still deeply entrenched in the ground, destined to flourish as the city's musicians helped bring their community back to life.

Speaking about jazz, Louis Armstrong once said, "What we play is life." The histories and passions of these musicians, in a city they love so much, show why they play so well. It was an honor to be able to spend time with them.

WHEN NOT PERFORMING

A MUSICIAN UNNAMED

$\mathcal{P}$rowling the neighborhood as we drove toward our scheduled meeting with Frogman Henry, Fred and I were discussing the unique nature of music in New Orleans. It seems as if everywhere in the city—uptown, downtown, back-o-town, Gert Town—kids are drumming on trash bins, street signs, or window frames at anytime, day or night. Others blow their trumpets, clarinets, or tubas while waiting for the buses and streetcars to take them to school. Still others sing and rap while walking home.

As we were closing in on our destination, we heard a faint sound of music that piqued our simultaneous curiosity. Not sure what it was, we both rolled down the windows to detect the source. Too intrigued to pass it by, we rounded several blocks in search. Then, in front of us, up on top of the levee, was a young man blowing his horn. We pulled over, parked the car, sat, and listened. It wasn't such great music, but there he was, practicing soulfully on his lonesome. The day was extremely hot, the air thick with humidity, and the young man had a towel covering his head as he faced the river. We sat listening and speculating as to why he chose the top of the levee in the midday heat: maybe his mother had grown tired of him, his practice might wake the baby, or the other children couldn't hear the TV. We speculated on all possibilities.

Then our conversation turned back to the subject of how this was a perfect example of why and how music is an ingrained part of our city. The singular soul up there practicing, performing, playing for his own pleasure or the pleasure of the passing ships, it didn't matter—he represented the importance of music to our city and culture. Whether it is because of the Mardi Gras parades, all of the festivals, or the fact that our poorly-insulated houses don't and can't contain the noise, music is everywhere. A day hardly goes by without hearing it in random locations, be it a parade, a party, a ribbon-cutting ceremony, or an impromptu jam session. Music is everywhere.

We finally decided to stop and ask this young man if we could take his picture, from the back so as to not identify him. He was to represent all of the boys and girls throughout New Orleans who have dreams of becoming a Marsalis, an Andrews, a Fats Domino, a John Rankin, and so on. Filling their need to express themselves through music, with music, they make all of us richer for it, too.

THERESA ANDERSSON

*H*ave a baby ten months prior and it's pretty safe to say where singer-songwriter Theresa Andersson is likely to be found when she is not performing—at the Algiers Point shotgun she shares with her husband, happily caring for young Elsie. Their house, like many older homes in the city, is in a perpetual state of renovation, nicely furnished but clearly the home of a toddler and her creative parents (Andersson's husband, Arthur Mintz, is a skilled puppeteer and musician).

The charming and attractive Andersson grew up on a farm in Sweden. Behind her New Orleans home is a lovely garden, a tranquil oasis that Andersson clearly cherishes. It is a natural space requiring very little tending. Coming back from long road trips, Andersson can pull a few weeds, do just a little digging, and feel right at home again.

An eighteen-year-old Andersson arrived in New Orleans in 1990. Violin firmly in hand, she was determined to experience the city's live music scene and its performers, both black and white. Straight from Sweden, she remembers walking out of the airport and being overpowered by the city's earthy, mildew-like smell (that was in January; imagine if she had arrived during the pungency of July—she may gone straight back to Scandinavia). For nine years, she played violin in a band and gained inspiration for her eventual solo career from Juanita Brooks, who told Andersson, "Baby, if you ever want to sing the right way, open up your body, turn your toes out, and give it all you got."

Andersson took the advice. Her career as a violinist, singer, and songwriter took off during the next decade. She played with the Neville Brothers, the Radiators, and the Meters and became a Jazz Fest regular. Allen Toussaint remains a major influence. She explains, "He represents so much of what is good about the music here." Not able to afford a tour of Europe with a full band, Andersson began experimenting with loop pedals to create her "One-Woman Show," singing while also playing her violin, guitar, record player, drums, and dulcimers. The YouTube video of her song "Na Na Na" has received nearly 1.5 million hits.

As the interview and photo shoot were ending, baby Elsie could be heard stirring in her nearby bedroom. Motherhood obviously agrees with Andersson, who has a soft and spiritual way about her. New Orleans is a long way from her native Sweden, "a lot different, a lot noisier." But with Elsie and her garden, it obviously agrees with her too.

GLEN DAVID ANDREWS

ew musicians are as closely identified with a New Orleans neighborhood as trombonist and singer Glen David Andrews is with Treme. It is possible that no other musician so clearly understands the redemptive powers of its streets, its people, and its music. It is no surprise then that Andrews chose his Treme church for his interview and photo shoot.

The mercurial Andrews is not easy to schedule. He calls during a lunch break to arrange an immediate meeting. For the interviewer, lunch ended suddenly for an opportunity to meet the irrepressible and talented trombonist in his neighborhood, in the church that he credits for straightening out his life. Andrews proves to be a passionate and animated conversationalist, a fierce defender of Treme and its street music ("if you got a problem with music, you ought not to be moving to the Treme"), and very open in describing the ups and downs of his complicated life.

Andrews was born in Treme in 1980. Neighborhood musicians literally brought him out of the womb: "When my mother was pregnant, Anthony 'Tuba Fats' Lacen came by and blew his horn outside the house. He said the sound of the tuba would induce labor. I was born the next day." Initially a drummer, he took up the trombone at age fourteen, encouraged by his younger cousin Troy (Trombone Shorty).

Without formal training, he learned playing on the streets of Treme and busking on Jackson Square. He provided back-up to Trombone Shorty and Shorty's brother, James, and performed with the New Birth Brass Band.

Andrews evacuated during Katrina. The storm was devastating, but Andrews claims it also helped him to refocus on what was really important and especially on his career. He began to headline more often, released several albums, and became a talented songwriter with an ear that mixes contemporary funk with traditional jazz, brass, and gospel sounds. He remains very much a part of the extended Andrews musical family: cousin to Troy, James, Revert, and another Glen (the latter two of Rebirth fame) and brother of Derrick Tabb (also of Rebirth).

Andrews freely admits to struggling with substance abuse and how, "but for music and the church (they saved my life)," he might be living on the streets. Politically engaged, in 2007 he sparked local and international outrage when the NOPD arrested him and Tabb at Tuba Fats Park in Treme for playing music during a funeral celebration for brass musician Kerwin James. Andrews is a survivor, coping with life day by day. He has the necessary education, proudly claiming that he studied at "the University of Treme."

JAMES ANDREWS

Outside his Valmont Street home in Uptown, jazz trumpeter James Andrews relaxes right outside in his backyard. It's a steaming New Orleans summer day, and Andrews is fresh off of playing a second line. The heat doesn't bother the seasoned veteran of the city's streets. It instead seems to energize him into passionate recollections of his extended family and their unique place in the city's music scene.

Andrews proves that, at least in New Orleans, six degrees of separation can be a gross overstatement. His family connections are deep and complex. Grandson of Jesse "Mr. Ooh-Poo-Pah-Doo," whose 1960 hit became a foundation of street funk, Andrews also claims kinship to Prince La La and Papoose Nelson, the Lasties, and a whole bunch of other Andrews, including brother Trombone Shorty and cousin Glen David. Born in Treme, Andrews grew up in the Ninth Ward with his grandfather and his neighbor, known only to Andrews as 'Toine. Only later did he figure out that the affable 'Toine was also known as Fats Domino.

Andrews built on these bloodlines to create his own blend of jazz, R&B, and brass-band music. He was an early disciple of Danny Barker, who had returned to the city determined to revive the city's brass band tradition. "Danny recruited me for a street band and told me and Leroy Jones and Michael White to be cool, just be cool, and listen to the old cats."

Andrews has tried to "combine the R&B of the Ninth Ward with the street music of the Treme." But he doesn't stop there: "New Orleans music has a lot of the Caribbean in it so I try to work in a hot popping bosa nova beat and a good horn line with a funk on top." That's a lot of music, resulting in albums such as the widely praised *Satchmo of the Ghetto*.

Andrews's duplex is full of new, post-storm furniture. His Mid-City home was destroyed after the levees broke. Andrews was among the first musicians to return and is an outspoken champion of the city's rebirth. Talkative, both serious and light-hearted, Andrews appreciates his heritage, saying, "I had no place else to go, I wasn't about to move to Omaha. In this city, we gotta remember what we done in the past is history, it's what we do in the future that's mystery. We can rebuild places, but we got soul and spirit and that's what we gotta work to save."

REVERT PEANUT ANDREWS

Long before the television show of the same name, Treme, the neighborhood just north of the French Quarter, enjoyed an iconic status as the epicenter of New Orleans street music, a vibrant scene resonating with second lines, Mardi Gras Indians, and Social Aid and Pleasure Clubs. The words to John Boutté's "Treme" sum it up as "Down in the Treme, just me and my baby, we're all going crazy, buck jumping and having fun." It is just the place to find talented street musician and trombonist Revert Peanut Andrews.

Andrews grew up and still lives in Treme along with his cousins James, Troy "Trombone Shorty," and Glen David. Originally scheduled to meet with Glen David, we found Peanut hanging out and grabbed the chance for a photograph. He moves comfortably through the neighborhood, carrying his trombone because you never know when you might need it. Everyone knows him and offers lots of waves and lots of "how ya' mom doin'"s. We take his photograph in front of Ruth's Cozy Corner, a corner store once run by his grandmother.

Peanut came by his heritage honestly, picking up the trombone while participating in Treme's many street parades. Like many in the neighborhood, he was mentored by Danny Barker, who had returned to New Orleans to spark a rebirth of the city's brass and marching traditions. Since 1993, Peanut has shared his talents with some of the city's best brass bands such as Dirty Dozen and Rebirth. Recently, he has played with Forgotten Souls Brass Band for the past two Jazz Fests and has been a prominent sideman to his cousin Glen David.

With his distinctive, gritty street sound, Andrews also has played with groups such as Widespread Panic and the bluesy North Mississippi Allstars. He had a role in the New Orleans music documentary *Make It Funky*. He has been a vocal advocate for street music in Treme and the Quarter. As the city and arrivistes to Treme try to curtail the traditional sounds of the neighborhood, Andrews objects, not understanding why someone would move there and then want to change what gives it character.

What the streets of New Orleans give, they also famously take away. When it came time to speak once again with Peanut for some final fact-checking, we found out that he was in jail for an unspecified offense. He is expected out soon. In the meantime, his family is doing what it can to keep his music alive—his cousin Glen David plays a nightly homage to him entitled "Whatever Happened to Peanut?"

LUCIEN BARBARIN

A fifth-generation New Orleans musician, distinguished jazz trombonist Lucien Barbarin speaks passionately about the need to preserve the city's traditional music. Nowhere is that need more acutely felt than on Bourbon Street with its rowdy clubs, drunken revelers, and tourist-infused musical scene.

That the elegant Barbarin would choose to be photographed in front of the Famous Door bar at Bourbon and Conti may seem strange. But his choice is a deliberate statement, reflecting his off-stage commitment to the preservation of jazz in historic venues such as those of the French Quarter. After his photograph, he retreats to the bar at the Royal Sonesta Hotel, home to a jazz club that "is trying to do the right thing and bring real jazz back to Bourbon."

Growing up in the city's Seventh Ward, Barbarin knew he wanted to play Bourbon Street ever since he found music at age six. There were plenty of influences to guide him in that direction. His great-uncle was Paul Barbarin, drummer for Kid Oliver and Louis Armstrong. He says, "Between listening to my Uncle Paul and parading through Treme with the second lines, I knew I had to do music." Barbarin's second cousin was jazz banjoist Danny Barker, who introduced him to the legendary Fairview Baptist Church Brass Band, incubator of talent such as Wynton and Branford Marsalis, Shannon Powell, and Michael White.

At age twenty, Barbarin realized his dream and played Bourbon Street with drummer June Gardner's band at the Famous Door. That gig led to others "back when Bourbon Street and the Quarter were about New Orleans music." Barbarin performed at Crazy Shirley's, the 500 Club, and La Strada, often playing two six-hour gigs per day. Playing with traditional jazz legends Percy and Willie Humphrey, he eventually became a regular at Preservation Hall.

Barbarin has gone on to international acclaim, touring with the likes of the Preservation Hall Jazz Band, Wynton Marsalis, Harry Connick Jr., and Lionel Hampton. But he always returns to Bourbon Street, even when not performing, relaxing in its bars and clubs and renewing friendships with fans and fellow musicians alike. He says, "I am a soldier for this music, and the front line to keep it alive is right down here in the Quarter."

DAVE BARTHOLOMEW

When legendary arranger and trumpeter Dave Bartholomew is not performing (which he still does on very rare occasions), chances are pretty high that he is being honored by some person or organization. Such was the case when he sat down for his photo in the lobby of the Roosevelt Hotel near Canal Street. At this luncheon, the New Orleans Arts Council was honoring Bartholomew, already a member of the Rock and Roll Hall of Fame, the Songwriters Hall of Fame, and the Louisiana Music Hall of Fame, for his contributions to the city's musical scene.

Bartholomew shows few effects of aging. His knee bothers him, but that is hardly surprising given his age. Dignified, almost regal, still with a great sense of humor, he holds court in the lobby as old friends drop by to pay their respects. Politicians pay homage and the hotel staff attends to his needs. It is the right place to be for a musician and composer who probably did more than anyone else to create the unique New Orleans R&B sound that many say gave birth to rock and roll.

Born upriver from New Orleans in Edgard, Louisiana, Bartholomew began playing the tuba and then changed to the trumpet. Using New Orleans as his home base, he played around the South and up and down the Mississippi with musicians such as Papa Celestin, Earl Palmer, and Red Tyler. While in the army, Bartholomew met Abraham Malone, who taught him how to write and arrange music.

After the war, he focused his efforts on writing and arranging. By the late 1940s, he had signed with Lew Chudd of Imperial Records. Not long afterward, in the Hideaway bar in New Orleans, he met an R&B singer and pianist from the Ninth Ward.

What followed was rock and roll history: Bartholomew and Fats Domino collaborating for nineteen consecutive albums that each sold one million copies, contributing "The Fat Man," "Ain't that a Shame," "Blue Monday," and "I'm Walkin'" to our collective musical memory. Besides Fats Domino, Bartholomew worked with artists such as Lloyd Price ("Lawdy Miss Clawdy"), Smiley Lewis ("Someday You'll Want Me"), and Shirley & Lee ("Let the Good Times Roll"). Bartholomew has more than four hundred songs in his catalogue and has sold hundreds of millions of records—he has come a long way from the North Galvez Street home where he used to rehearse with Fats in the back studio while his wife ran a beauty shop in the front.

Back in the 1930s and 1940s, the Roosevelt was favored by the white establishment and was a kind of place that Bartholomew would never have been allowed to frequent as a patron. It is not far from Cosimo Matassa's J&M Recording Studio, where Bartholomew used to work with Fats. Years later, Bartholomew has made the short journey around the corner, having changed musical history in the process.

UNCLE LIONEL BATISTE

Few New Orleans faces are as widely known as Uncle Lionel Batiste's (not to mention his last name, which he shares with other great musical Batistes such as Alvin, Harold, Russell, and Jonathan). Bass drummer and vocalist of the Treme Brass Band, Uncle Lionel missed few opportunities to play in the streets, second lines, jazz funerals, and festivals—his lifeblood. And with his trim figure, mustache, sunglasses, shined shoes, and hats (especially his Treme Brass Band hat), the debonair Batiste was instantly recognizable. If you walked down a New Orleans street with Uncle Lionel, especially in Treme, you wouldn't lack for friends.

Batiste lived in a high-rise right off of Frenchmen Street across from Snug Harbor. His living room was a museum of his life, with drums, sashes, umbrellas, and photos of his many performances scattered around. Boxes of shoes were everywhere, which he justified by saying, "Gotta have good shoes when you lead a parade." And in his trademark style, Uncle Lionel wore his watch just below his knuckles so that "I always have time on my hands."

The youngest of eleven children, Batiste was born in 1931 in the family home at the corner of St. Philip and St. Claude in the Treme neighborhood. He grew up surrounded by musicians and street music, including George Lewis, Smiley Lewis, and Alphonse Picou. His first drum was the family washtub, but only after it sprang a leak and he claimed it as his own. At age seven, his first band was the Original Sixth Ward Kazoo Band. That launched a lifetime of parading with the Olympia Brass Band, the Tuxedo, the O'Howard, and the Liberty.

Son of a blacksmith and no stranger to hard work, the energetic Uncle Lionel worked all sorts of odd jobs: float-maker, bowling pin-setter, embalmer, bricklayer, and praline delivery man, to name a few. But there was always time for music. He helped start the Treme Brass Band with his lifelong friend, snare drummer Benny Jones. While best known for his drumming, he also played the kazoo, whipping it out of his pocket when the spirit moved him. He sang in a gravelly, traditional style and released an album accompanied by musicians such as Evan Christopher, Lars Edegran, and Mark Brooks.

Uncle Lionel's distinctive look and musical style rewarded him with spots on television shows and commercials. And his face remains signature. He was featured on Terrance Osborne's "Say Uncle" 2010 Jazz Fest Congo Square poster. And even though Facebook arrived after his youth, there is, naturally, a page dedicated to Uncle Lionel Batiste, everybody's favorite street drummer.

Uncle Lionel died July 8, 2012, after a brief illness. Within hours of his passing, Kermit Ruffins and Rebirth Brass Band took to the streets with Uncle Lionel's fans to honor his life and music.

TERENCE BLANCHARD

*O*n an elegant home on St. Charles Avenue lives Terence Blanchard, in a place where he takes quiet sanctuary from his busy schedule as a prolific trumpeter, bandleader, and composer. The sounds of the streetcar rumbling up the neutral ground are muffled in the background. The home is elevated, the living room almost in the trees; the house is cool and elegant, much like the original music of the gracious Blanchard.

Catching up with Blanchard was not easy. With projects all over the world, the man who has written more film scores than any jazz musician in history is frequently not in town. But the articulate and thoughtful Blanchard steadfastly returns home whenever he can, living Uptown near Audubon Park and Tulane University with his wife, Robin, and four children. The house is graciously furnished, with a grand piano in the living room and Blanchard's five Grammy Awards an added touch on the mantle.

An only child born in 1962, Blanchard grew up around music, "mostly sacred, my father sang in the church choir and knew some opera." While still in grade school, he was exposed to the trumpet of Alvin Acorn who played with Kid Ory. He explains, "That gave me the bug, the passion." Blanchard studied with Ellis Marsalis at NOCCA, attended Rutgers to study jazz, and by 1980 was touring with Lionel Hampton. In 1982, he joined Art Blakely's Jazz Messengers. Later in the eighties, he worked with Donald Harrison Jr., both influential contributors to the jazz resurgence of that decade.

Blanchard performed on two movie soundtracks for director Spike Lee. He continued to work in Hollywood with Lee and others such as director George Lucas. Blanchard has played in nearly fifty film scores, forty of which he composed. Included in his compositional body of work is the score for Lee's award-winning *When the Levees Broke: a Requiem in Four Acts*. His hard-bop style combined with distinctive elements of African fusion has made him one of the most successful and recognizable jazz trumpeters in the world.

With all this, it would have been easy for Blanchard to leave his hometown behind. But he has remained loyal to "a place where the music is so vast, I can't begin to explain it." Like so many others, he was deeply impacted by Katrina, telling *Jazz Police* in an interview after the storm that although the city's musical roots were threatened, "We are going to work hard to help jazz and New Orleans flourish once again." His commitment to those goals has produced tangible results. As Artistic Director of the Thelonius Monk Institute of Jazz since 2000, he was influential in bringing the Institute from Los Angeles to the campus of New Orleans's Loyola University in 2007.

MIA BORDERS

Magazine Street in New Orleans does hip well. And on "Mag," the hip diner Slim Goodies is run by friends of bluesy-rock and soul singer Mia Borders, herself undeniably, yes, hip. So it is a natural place to meet for morning coffee with the youthful and, given the time of day, surprisingly animated Borders.

Borders is one of those New Orleans musicians on the verge, recognized by the city's musical community as an emerging artist who could be the next big thing. She is bright and ambitious. Accompanied by her manager, she is aware that in music, when it's your time, it's your time.

Only in her mid-twenties, Borders has already traveled a long and winding musical road—and an unusual one, even by New Orleans standards. A native of the city, she had plenty of music in her childhood with a grandfather who played the trumpet and professional parents who exposed her to their record player before teaching her to walk. Composing at a young age and also picking up the guitar, Borders went to Taft, a prep school in Connecticut—maybe not the customary launching pad for a New Orleans blues singer. A guitar solo her senior year helped her overcome stage fright, but not so much that she decided to be a musician. In 2005, before Katrina, she was planning on attending film school in Georgia.

The storm changed all that, and, after a less-than-enthusiastic evacuation to Atlanta, she returned to her hometown in January 2006.

But still no full-time music. Borders enrolled at Loyola in 2006 and graduated with an English degree in 2010. She played a couple of gigs per month then, worked as a paralegal, and formed a band with some colleagues. Planning to go to grad school, in 2010, she made the decision: "I am going to make a living playing music." And since then, Borders has done just that. She has released a couple of well-received albums, plays at clubs all over town, toured extensively, and made a splash at Austin's South by Southwest festival. With her sensual and distinctive voice, which she combines with a strong rhythm guitar, Borders is getting it done in her hometown, saying, "I really can't imagine, don't want to live anywhere else."

At her 2011 Jazz Fest appearance, Borders more than held her own on a bill that featured Robert Plant, Jeff Beck, and Wyclef Jean. But she added something that none of them could. At Taft, Borders was a member of an all-female a cappella group, Hydrox. From the Gentilly Stage, Borders gave an animated shout-out to a former Hydrox in the audience. It can't be confirmed, but it may be the only prep school shout-out in the storied history of Jazz Fest.

JOHN BOUTTÉ

Treme has always been home to John Boutté. The diminutive jazz singer is a seventh-generation Creole, living in the shotgun cottage that his great-grandfather built next door to the house that his father erected and where he grew up. On one of those New Orleans summer days where, as writer Tom Robbins says, "The heat and humidity seem to stop the clocks and make time stand still," Boutté relaxes in his lushly landscaped backyard. He practices the trumpet, shows off a fishing rod, and talks pretty much non-stop in a unique, lyrical style.

The inside of Boutté's house is equally eclectic. A 105-year-old family piano is in the living room. Photographs of several generations of relatives are randomly scattered, hung the old-fashioned way using wire attached to the ceiling. Art by famed New Orleans painter and sculptor John T. Scott graces the wall. Refrigerator magnets track Boutté's international travels. And his freezer is full of Louisiana food, befitting his talents as a skilled cook.

One of ten children, Boutté was born in 1959 and grew up surrounded by music, from the raucous gospel shouts of the Sanctified Church next door to the street sounds of the Eureka Brass Band. He claims, "Best part [was] we had no AC so I could hear everything." After playing in his high school marching band, Boutté at first went in a direction away from music. He graduated from Xavier University, served four years as a lieutenant in the army, and returned to the city to work for a credit union.

A chance encounter with Stevie Wonder changed everything. Wonder had borrowed Boutté's piano for a rehearsal. After hearing Boutté's almost angelic voice, Wonder encouraged him to sing full-time. The very next day, he quit the credit union, stopped shaving, threw away his neck ties, and moved to Europe to be with his sister Lillian, herself a renowned jazz and gospel singer. After honing his talents overseas, he returned to New Orleans to launch a successful jazz, R&B, gospel, and blues career.

Charismatic, profoundly independent, and outspoken, Boutté keeps a tight control on his career. After Katrina, he was the first in his family to return. "I didn't lose anything because I never worry about stuff. I got my music, I own it, and no damn storm was gonna take that away." In 2012, Boutté captured a national audience as a result of appearances on HBO's *Treme* and the selection of his music as the show's highly recognizable theme song. Fame hasn't changed him. He remains down in Treme, close to friends, family, and the neighborhood he loves.

LEAH CHASE

*I*nterviewing and photographing New Orleans musicians all over town is a pretty good gig in and of itself. But when jazz singer Leah Chase chooses to be photographed in her mother's famous Creole restaurant, Dooky Chase, and she has a plate of fried chicken and sides made up just for you, that's about as good as it gets.

The affable and warm-spirited Chase comes by her hospitality naturally. Her parents have run their Fifth Ward restaurant since the 1940s, welcoming civil rights activists in the 1960s and politicians of all stripes ever since. The walls feature a dazzling display of African-American art. Chase works in the restaurant with her eighty-nine-year-old mother who "is not slowing down anytime soon."

Chase grew up listening to the music of the city on the streets of Treme. Like a lot of the city's musicians, she didn't have air-conditioning so "we sat out on the porch and watched the parades." She majored in classical music at Loyola and attended Juilliard for a year. After migrating to Los Angeles, Chase returned to New Orleans in 1980. Her sister had died prematurely and her devastated family needed her to help in the restaurant. Encouraged by Dolores Marsalis, wife of Ellis, Chase sang at a benefit and soon was a regular in the city's many jazz venues.

Working in the restaurant and teaching music at Tulane, Loyola, and the University of New Orleans, Chase has her mother's energy. Her intimate and gentle style allows her a special connection with her audiences; "I want them to see inside my mind, to feel the life I've lived." Displaced by Katrina, she put things into a new perspective, explaining, "I used to get so nervous before I sang—Jazz Fest was a nightmare. But after the storm, I had no money, no job, no place to live. We weren't sure if Dooky Chase would even reopen. How hard could singing be?"

The restaurant did re-open, and Chase now lives in a shotgun right across from the parking lot. As she relaxes at a table after lunch, her mother still at work in the kitchen, Chase relishes the unique, ubiquitous sound of New Orleans. "We're different," she says. "We hear music in the womb; it just swallows us up. And we are so laid back, we celebrate everything and we use music to do it. And we don't judge, we don't tell you how to play, and what comes through despite all our problems is our joy of life."

EVAN CHRISTOPHER

On Calhoun Street near Tulane University, not far from jazz clarinetist Evan Christopher's Broadmoor home, is a coffee shop, The First Cup Café, owned by Christopher's good friend, Mo. Christopher uses the Café as his office, and Mo accepts delivery of his mail and packages while Christopher is on the road. During the interview and photo shoot, Mo helps to guard Christopher's privacy by shutting the blinds and telling customers, "We're closed."

Christopher sets up in the corner, his laptop at the ready. There is a persistent knock on the door even after Mo says again, "We're closed." It's UPS with a package for Christopher. He notes the Bulgarian return address and smiles. It is an antique clarinet, one from the 1930s and 1940s that Christopher has been expecting for months while it was tied up in customs. He carefully unpacks it, runs his fingers gently on its burnished wood, and observes how slowly he will need to introduce it to the city's humidity.

Born in 1969, Christopher is a native Californian. He began playing clarinet at age eleven, trained at the Idyllwild Arts Academy, and eventually graduated from California State University in Long Beach. After touring in New Orleans with A. J. Croce (son of Jim), he officially moved to the city in 1994. When he arrived, he discovered that after the death of Willie Humphrey a few months prior, there were no living clarinet players in the early New Orleans style. A disciple of great traditional jazz clarinetists

Sidney Bechet, Johnny Dodds, and Lorenzo Tio Jr. among others, Christopher set about to fill the absence. He succeeded admirably.

Over the next eighteen years, Christopher moved from New Orleans twice: once voluntarily to San Antonio for two years to play with the Jim Cullum Jazz Band and once involuntarily to France after Katrina destroyed his home. In Paris, he formed Django à la Créole, a fusion of "Gypsy" jazz and New Orleans texture. He returned to Louisiana in 2008 to teach at the University of New Orleans and to play with musicians such as Tom McDermott, Lucien Barbarin, and Marcus Roberts. He remains determined to explore and explain the musicology of the city, contributing his "Riffing on Tradition" blog to the website NolaVie. He claims, "I want to be an advocate for the language of New Orleans music."

The trim and fit Christopher is known for his swaggering, charismatic performances, with the unique style he has created as a New Orleans-Creole clarinetist. Off stage, though, he is shy, serious, and deeply engaged while discussing the historical roots of New Orleans music, "a language of its own that varies even among the city's neighborhoods." He is "fascinated how musicians from the Treme [neighborhood] can sound so different than those from the Ninth Ward even though they are only a couple of miles apart." He then plays a few notes on his new instrument, a worthy heir of the great clarinetists of his adopted hometown.

JON CLEARY

Sharing a cup of afternoon tea with R&B and funk musician Jon Cleary in his Burgundy Street home is very English. That he lives in the Faubourg Marigny, one of the city's oldest neighborhoods, is very New Orleanian. Both of which make perfect sense in meeting with the ultra-talented Cleary, who was born in England but by now is from New Orleans.

Cleary relaxes in his old, rambling home, its occasional clutter a reflection of his 1960s-musician's lifestyle and lots of time spent on the road. He reflects on growing up in England with New Orleans and its R&B music embedded in his soul, saying, "Getting here was always my great ambition." His uncle, an artist and musician, was largely responsible, sending Cleary long illustrated letters from his New Orleans home; describing the allure of Professor Longhair, the Mardi Gras Indians, and the Funky Butt Lounge; and supplementing these epistles with forty-five rpm records he brought back to England and to which Cleary listened constantly.

It all proved irresistible to a young Cleary. When he turned seventeen, he caught the first plane from the UK to New Orleans for a vacation and ended up staying in the city for two years. Upon arriving, he went straight from the airport to the Maple Leaf Bar, where the first New Orleans musician he met was the eccentric pianist James Booker, who lived above the Maple Leaf. Cleary moved in around the corner,

took a job painting the Maple Leaf ("I was paid in beer and no cover") and began to absorb what he could by listening to Booker and Roosevelt Sykes, who "used to hang out in the bar during the day and play while I painted."

Forced by immigration laws to return to the UK after two years, Cleary took what he had learned in New Orleans and started his own R&B band in England. But he knew he had to get back to Louisiana to find the kind of musicians that he needed. He returned and did sideman work with James Singleton, Smokey Johnson, Johnny Adams, George Porter, Johnny Vidacovich, Irving Charles, and others, and eventually hooked up with Walter "Wolfman" Washington for a couple of years. He started to write; formed his own band, the Absolute Monster Gentlemen; and developed such a reputation for distinctively blending traditional R&B, soul, and funk that he is now a sought after accompanist for musicians such as Bonnie Raitt, John Scofield, and Taj Mahal.

Cleary has a studio with the usual bells and whistles of modern recording technology downstairs in his Marigny home. But he is very much a traditionalist, arguing that music is a product of soul, imagination, and emotion, and that "machinery and computers are an adjunct to the experience, not its reason." It is the kind of attitude one would expect from a musician who long ago adopted a city like New Orleans as his real home.

HARRY CONNICK SR.

Spend thirty challenging years as the District Attorney in crime-ridden New Orleans and you will need an occasional refuge, a place to retreat from politics and to get lost in music. Harry Connick Sr. has both at his gracious Broadmoor home and the New Orleans clubs where he has fronted as a vocalist for some of the city's best musicians.

Greeting his visitors on his front porch, where he retrieves a gift left for him by a grateful Catholic priest, Connick is surrounded in his home by eclectic artwork, family photos, haphazardly-strewn books, and mementoes of his legal and musical career. Although widely traveled, he remains strongly rooted in his neighborhood, living since 1997 in a house next door to where he and his wife Anita raised their two children, Suzanna and Harry Jr., and not far from the Plum Street home in which he grew up.

Connick was raised in a large Catholic family and remains deeply religious. After graduating from St. Aloysius High School, he served in the navy during World War II. He was a crew member on a Higgins boat, manufactured (where else?) in New Orleans. He has a small model of his former boat prominently displayed in his dining room. He returned to the city after the war and with his wife, Anita, operated two record stores while they both attended law school. Practicing criminal law, in 1973 Connick defeated Jim Garrison of JFK-conspiracy fame to become the parish's District Attorney. Anita enjoyed her own great success as one of the city's first female judges and eventually as a member of the Louisiana Supreme Court before her premature death in 1981.

Like many New Orleanians, Connick grew up listening to music, with a fondness for the big-band standards of the 1930s and 1940s. But until he was sixty-five, it had always been a hobby, a way to relax from the pressures of his legal career. It was only after his son Harry Jr.'s career took off that Connick Sr. first took the stage as a musician. He joined Harry Jr. in Las Vegas singing some of his old favorites. Word of the vocal talents of the "Singing DA" got back home and soon he was in demand to perform for benefits and in local clubs. This late-in-life "professional" musician soon fronted for some of the city's best, including David Torkanowsky, Matt Perrine, and Craig Klein, playing in venerated venues such as Tipitina's.

"Only in New Orleans" is probably an over-used phrase. But there aren't many cities where someone could have combined as many successful roles as Connick: longtime prosecutor, husband of Anita, father and mentor of Harry Jr. and Suzanna, and musician in his own right. Connick appreciates this good fortune, saying, "Music is such a special tradition here, I am blessed to help pass it along."

SUSAN COWSILL

New Orleans is like a secret garden, a place where regeneration and rebirth is the norm. And in New Orleans, maybe its most secret garden is Algiers, right across the Mississippi River. Singer Susan Cowsill, who lives in the quirky neighborhood with her husband, Russ Broussard, and daughter, Miranda, thinks so.

Cowsill's home is happy and relaxed, with neighbors dropping by for wine and stray cats making their presence known. It's the kind of place where someone as closely identified with the 1960s as Cowsill is would call home. But it also has a post-Katrina feel, with a strong contrast between the lots of new stuff and the old that recalls the toll the storm took. In Cowsill's case, that toll was deeply personal.

A navy kid with five brothers, Cowsill was the youngest member of the 1960s-pop band, the Cowsills, one of rock's first family bands and the inspiration for the *Partridge Family*. After a series of hits, the band broke up in 1972, but not until young Susan had sung with Dean Martin and danced with Buddy Ebsen. Occasionally re-uniting with her brothers during the next two decades, Susan honed her guitar and songwriting skills, mostly while living in Los Angeles. As a member of the roots band the Continental Drifters, she moved to New Orleans when the band relocated there in 1993. She explains, "I was pregnant at the time, just loaded a U-Haul and moved east. It felt like the *Grapes of Wrath* in reverse."

Intending to stay only a couple of years, Cowsill developed an affinity for her new hometown, saying, "After L.A., where no one has any roots, this place feels so secure." She has flourished with a variety of musical identities, playing with a reunited Cowsills, her own band, and Paul Sanchez's Rollin' Road Show. In 2003, she married Russ Broussard, one of the city's best drummers. Hurricane Katrina destroyed everything in their Mid-City home, and they drifted for four months before deciding to return. They moved back in January 2006, when Susan confronted the storm's real horror. Her brother Barry had not evacuated. After a series of voicemails from him right after Katrina, suddenly she heard nothing more. His body was discovered in the river on the day after she returned, the exact circumstances of his death unknown. Susan is convinced that he committed suicide after a deeply troubled life.

Even with these struggles, Cowsill remains optimistic, a vital part of the resurgent New Orleans music scene post-storm. As she told the *Huffington Post*, Hurricane Katrina was a "muse and metaphor for life. Yes, all these terrible things can happen, but you can still be a happy person."

DANCING MAN 504

*P*eople in New Orleans form identity from all sorts of things—music, oysters, crawfish, parades, Creole cottages, the Saints, and, for some reason, the city's area code, 504. There is a jazz record label, 504 Records; a hip-hop group, 504 Boyz; and Rapper 504. There is also Darryl Young, known as Dancing Man 504, who since Katrina has taken to the streets of the city as an ambassador for second line dance and culture.

The athletic Young performs in the streets of New Orleans, randomly appearing at second lines, festivals, concerts, and funerals. He is extremely fit, and the city's steamy climate does not slow him down at all. On an August day, just after he had danced seemingly non-stop at the Satchmo Summer Festival, the otherwise animated Young relaxes at his Broadmoor home, which he also uses as an occasional teaching studio.

A Ninth Ward native, Young played high school basketball and football and was "not really into music." After returning to New Orleans post-Katrina, he was determined to make a difference in the lives of the city's children. "I wanted to do something about the crime, to give kids an alternative," he says. He seized upon second line dancing, which he defines as "structured chaos, an outlet to help people expel pent up energy." Young founded "Heal 2 Toe," a teaching program where he works with brass bands to expose kids to second line dance and the city's cultural heritage. So far, he has worked with more than two thousand children. He also sponsors an adult fitness program, BrassXCise, to incorporate brass and elements of second line dancing into physical wellbeing.

Young took to the streets to spread the word. He liked to dance to narrow the gap between tourists and locals. "The people gave me my name, that's dancing man, and it stuck." His street dancing performances gained a YouTube following, he paraded across the Brooklyn Bridge with the Jambalaya Brass Band, and he led three hundred French children in a second line. In New Orleans, he has danced with the Soul Rebels, Shamarr Allen, the Treme Brass Band, and the Kinfolk Brass Band.

There is an organic "Where's Waldo" way about Dancing Man's performances. You never know where he is likely to show up, be it at Jazz Fest, Frenchmen Street, the streets of Treme, or Audubon Park. But he remains passionately consistent about his message: "Through second lining, we can break down barriers; we have a responsibility to use our culture to help our kids." In 504, Young has put his feet where his mouth is.

JEREMY DAVENPORT

New Orleans streets have always resonated with the sound of music in parades, festivals, and second line celebrations. Its music is also found in the city's clubs, famous and infamous, fancy and informal. Trumpeter Jeremy Davenport is a regular in one of those clubs, the Davenport Lounge in the Ritz Carlton Hotel on Canal Street. He lives in the hotel, which allows him to "commute by elevator," avoiding daily hassles when he is not on stage. He also has his own rehearsal space in the hotel's old French Quarter Bar. On the day he was photographed, the amiable and talkative Davenport opened the floor-to-ceiling windows in this rehearsal space, allowing the noise of the Quarter to drift in while he described "this amazingly fertile and welcoming environment called New Orleans."

Davenport loves the intersection of his personal and professional lives in one hotel and its "big room" lounge. His trumpet never far from his side, he can get away without ever having to go outside. He worked hard for the opportunity—when three hundred days of annual touring began to lose its charm, Davenport heard rumors that the Ritz might be opening on Canal, and ever mindful of New Orleans tradition, he envisioned performing regularly in a hotel club that evoked the old Blue Room in the city's Roosevelt Hotel. His persistent lobbying and popular, traditional jazz style led to the gig, now one of the most well-attended in the city.

Growing up in St. Louis, Davenport was introduced to jazz by his musical parents. His father was a trombonist with the St. Louis Symphony, and his mother was a voice teacher for forty-five years. When Davenport was twelve, he met Wynton Marsalis, who tried to convince him to move to New Orleans. Davenport's mother, his educator, was having none of that, "not until I finished high school." But Marsalis soon got his way. After high school, Davenport moved to New York to attend the Manhattan School of Music. He reestablished contact with Wynton, who this time successfully convinced him to move to New Orleans to train with Wynton's father, legendary jazz musician and instructor Ellis Marsalis. Ellis refined Davenport's trumpet into a more traditional sound, resulting in a four-year stint for Davenport playing with the scion of another New Orleans musical family, Harry Connick Jr.

Davenport is also an outspoken and opinionated advocate for the city's musicians. Appreciative of his own opportunities, he argues that New Orleans still needs more venues that pay a decent wage to its most treasured resource, "the musicians."

QUINT DAVIS

With Jazz Fest scheduled to take place in a few weeks, there really is very little quiet-time for an interview and photo shoot in the life of festival producer and director Quint Davis. But Davis is a master of time-management, the one most heavily responsible for the famously clockwork-like Jazz Fest performances ("the real secret is getting them off-stage on time"). On a spring Saturday afternoon, he graciously takes an hour out of his 24/7 lifestyle to welcome us into his modern-style home right on the edge of Bayou St. John.

Davis is colorful, confident, and creative. His personality is larger-than-life, exactly the kind you need to balance the demands of competing constituencies, thousands of musicians, and an opinionated Jazz Fest fan base ("it's amazing how many years in a row I have been able to 'ruin' Jazz Fest"). Since its creation in 1970, Davis's enthusiasm, disciplined attention to the bottom-line, and imagination have transformed a regional heritage festival into an internationally-known, iconic event.

Born in 1947, Davis is a New Orleans native. His father, Arthur, was a noted architect: designer of the Superdome, the New Orleans Arena, and numerous downtown hotels. As a teenager, Davis embraced New Orleans street culture with its second lines and jazz funerals. He also had an early affinity for African music. After leaving college in Illinois in the late 1960s, Davis returned to New Orleans to live the lifestyle of that era, playing in a psychedelic band and looking the part. He went to Tulane for ethnomusicology. He says, "I wanted to make a career out of my passion." It was there that he was contacted by producer and festival organizer George Wein, who was looking for a young New Orleanian to help him book local acts for the inaugural Jazz and Heritage Festival, to be held in Congo Square in 1970.

Davis's relationship with Wein lit the fire in his career. Traveling extensively, he road-managed B. B. King, Muddy Waters, Chuck Berry, Fats Domino, and Duke Ellington. At the urging of Wein, he sought out an obscure and destitute piano player, Henry Roeland Byrd, and with the help of his then-girlfriend, Allison Miner, orchestrated Professor Longhair's comeback. All the while, he produced and directed Jazz Fest (adding Essence Festival in 1995), not always without controversy, but always consistent with his lifelong passion for the city's music.

With all the moving parts in his life, Davis's home provides him valuable respite. But it very much reflects who he is, with collections of folk art, African art and sculpture, and musical memorabilia everywhere. Davis claims only in New Orleans "could I have done what I have been able to do." Although he doesn't sing or play an instrument, Davis has done more than enough to be considered part of the New Orleans musical community.

FATS DOMINO

New Orleans has had its Fat Man ever since Fats Domino burst upon the national R&B and rock scene in 1949 when he recorded for Dave Bartholomew in Cosimo Matassa's Rampart Street studio. And Fats has always had his New Orleans, the city where he was born and raised—always in the Lower Ninth Ward, where by the 1980s, he vowed to stay put, not leaving to be inducted into the Rock and Roll Hall of Fame as a charter member or to play for President Clinton at the Kennedy Center. What fame and politics could not accomplish, however, Katrina did. To the horror of a transfixed nation, Fats was reported missing, lost among the ensuing chaos. Unknown to the rest of the country, he had been evacuated from the roof of his home by the Coast Guard, taken to the Superdome, and eventually ended up in Houston.

Fats no longer lives in New Orleans proper. He is with his daughter in a gated West Bank community. Still genial but slowed a little by age, he looks distractedly out her living room window, conveying a wistful feeling of loss. Only a few miles from his old Caffin Street home and studio, he clearly misses his friends, his food, and his city.

Antoine Domino, born in 1928 as the youngest of eight children, has a mystical bond with New Orleans and the Lower Ninth. His Creole family lived on Jourdan Avenue, where he grew up around his extended family, soaked in music. Quitting school after fourth grade, he practiced the piano incessantly in the garage on an old upright with rusty keys. His first performance was at his sister Philomena's house, converted into a neighborhood bar with fifteen-cent beer. His brother-in-law, Harrison Verret, took him to Verret's regular gig at the Court of Two Sisters in the Quarter. Domino dazzled the white patrons with a raucous boogie-woogie, leading to more gigs at places such as the Hideaway bar and the Robin Hood. Band leader Billy Diamond christened the five-foot-five Domino (who had a fondness for ham hocks and pigs feet) as "Fats," predestining him to be as famous as Fats Waller.

Working first with Bartholomew, Fats was Elvis before Elvis, a courageous live performer whose concerts broke the barriers of segregation. He was the first black musician to sell more than one million singles with "Ain't That a Shame." Until the 1960s, he was a fixture on the charts and then spent the next twenty years touring. He married Rosemary Hall from the Lower Ninth, where he continued to live until the storm, and where he always felt most at home.

In his daughter's house, Fats is surrounded by the few gold records and occasional piece of furniture, such as a Cadillac-finned couch, that were not destroyed by Katrina. He sits at his piano. At first, he appears unable to remember lyrics or music. But with very little coaxing, he soon is ripping it up, the music in his DNA, sounding like he was twenty again and playing in the city's clubs. He may not be in New Orleans, but there is still plenty of New Orleans left in the Fat Man.

DAVID DOUCET

Cajuns are many things, modest being one of them. Such certainly is the case for guitarist David Doucet, who stores his two Grammys as bookends on the top shelf of an otherwise out-of-the-way bookcase. He laughs, "I used to keep them on top of the TV, but flat-screens sort of killed that deal."

Photographed in the kitchen of his Uptown home, the talkative and friendly Doucet does not live in Lafayette as many assume. Lead guitarist of the Grammy Award-winning band Beausoleil, Doucet is the younger brother of the band's leader, Michael, and has deep roots in Louisiana's Cajun country.

Doucet first began playing Cajun music with Beausoleil in 1976, when David was in college and then graduate school, where he earned a masters in English. In the early 1980s, he moved to New Orleans looking for work. Fluent in Greek and Latin, he wryly noted, "Not much work for a philologist in Lafayette." Apparently, there wasn't much in New Orleans, either. Instead, Doucet worked at the 1984 World's Fair, playing three sets six times per week.

Doucet fell in love with the city for "its scale, its intimacy, its attitude, not to mention its airport."

Doucet never moved back to Lafayette. He immersed himself in the city's music, listening to Snooks Eaglin at Tyler's and frequenting Tastee Donuts with Earl King. Like many of the city's musicians, Doucet embraces different traditions. Influenced by Doc Watson, Mississippi John Hurt, and John Fahey, Doucet developed a unique style, flatpicking with Beausoleil and fingerpicking for his own enjoyment. Musically curious, he continues to experiment with influences as diverse as the field recordings of Alan Lomax and modern Hawaiian acoustic guitarists such as Sonny Chillingworth.

Touring nearly two hundred days per year, Doucet returns as often as possible to his Uptown home to relax, to ride his bike, and to enjoy the Try Me Coffee that he loves and can only get in New Orleans. Doucet is also a talented cook, who nonetheless insists that, when touring, his contract stipulate "no Cajun food; I pretty much had to do that after the pineapple gumbo in Atlanta."

DR. JOHN

Trying to pin down the spiritual and magical Dr. John for his photograph was never going to be easy. Nor should it have been. Capturing the smoky image of a legend is meant to be tough. The pianist has created a voodoo-like persona deeply rooted in the city's African, Haitian, and Cuban cultural traditions—mystery is mandated, open and direct contact is not.

Dr. John eventually agreed to be photographed on the porch of the New Orleans home where he lives, but only on the condition that the location not be disclosed. Enjoying his first cup of coffee, the gentlemanly and dignified Dr. John speaks softly and slowly in his distinctive "dis" and "dat" style. A fierce guardian of New Orleans and its traditions, he is at once angry about the loss of the Gulf's wetlands, sorrowful about the deaths of friends such as Willie Tee and Wardell Quezergue, and proud of the city's young musical talent such as Trombone Shorty ("everybody here be related; Shorty, he is Jesse Hill's grandson").

Dr. John was born Mac Rebennack in 1941, the son of the owner of Rebennack's Appliance Co. on Gentilly Boulevard. He attended Jesuit High School and played guitar until his left ring finger was shot when he defended a high school classmate. Rebennack shifted his talents to the piano and was a fixture in the city's 1950s music scene, "playing a lot of R&B, but we called it race music." In 1963, he moved to Los Angeles, where he became a popular session musician, backing up the likes of Cher and Canned Heat.

But New Orleans was never far from his mind. In 1967, he created the Dr. John persona, based on one of the city's legendary nineteenth-century voodoo practitioners. Dr. John soon became Dr. John the Night Tripper, the vehicle for a wild stage-show that blended funk, R&B, jazz, and voodoo. A prolific songwriter, Dr. John's musical evolution has never stopped. Transcending genres from New Orleans R&B to funk to pop to jazz to rock, he was inducted into the Rock and Roll Hall of Fame in 2011. His influence spans generations—the annual Bonnaroo Music and Arts Festival takes its name from his 1974 *Desitively Bonnaroo* album.

Music writer John Swenson has described his friend Rebennack as an "ancient mariner" who "understands more about the relationship between spirit, culture, magic, and music in New Orleans" than anyone else. Talking to Rebennack on the porch of his secret, undisclosed home, it is easy to see Swenson's perspective. Politicized by Katrina, Rebennack's passionate crusade since the storm has been for the safety of the Gulf and its wetlands. But his is not the cool calculation of an ecologist; it arises from his spiritual, magical voodoo traditions that are deeply respectful of nature and very much part of who Dr. John is.

LIONEL FERBOS

For most musicians born in 1911, at least for those who are fortunate enough to still be with us, finding a time when they are not performing should be an easy task, presumably with 24/7 availability. Not so in the case of jazz trumpeter Lionel Ferbos, the oldest active jazz musician in the world (as of this writing), who is not available on Saturday night when he plays his weekly gig at the Palm Court in the French Quarter.

Ferbos lives in Pontchartrain Park with his daughter, Sylvia. His wife, Marguerite, to whom he was married for seventy-five years, died in 2009. Ferbos looks great, claiming that music is still one way of getting out and staying young (and who can argue with that?). Trumpet by his side as he relaxes on the couch, the well-mannered Ferbos is dressed in a suit and tie, hat nearby, disdainful of younger musicians who "dress so sloppy and don't understand how good clothes can be as important as good music."

Born in the largely Creole Seventh Ward, Ferbos had asthma as a child. As a result, his parents discouraged him from playing a wind instrument. After seeing an all girl's band, including trumpeters, Ferbos convinced his parents that he should be allowed to play, arguing, "if girls can play it, so can I" (modern feminism was evidently not yet an influence when Ferbos was a young man). As a result of his lessons with Paul Chaligny, who insisted that his students be able to read music, Ferbos does not improvise, but instead reads song sheets and writes out his trumpet solos. Like his father and grandfather before him, he also spent time working as a sheet metal worker.

In the 1920s, Ferbos played with Captain John Handy's Louisiana Shakers. In the 1930s, he was a member of the Works Progress Administration Band. In the 1940s and 1950s, he played with the Creole band the Mighty Four. In the 1960s, he played with Herbert Leary's dance orchestra. In the 1970s, he joined Lars Edegran's New Orleans Ragtime Orchestra. And since 1991, he has been a weekly regular at the Palm Court, even returning after Katrina severely damaged his home and he lost most of his possessions.

There are many ways to measure Ferbos's extraordinary longevity. Born the same year as Tennessee Williams and Lucille Ball, he is only ten years younger than Louis Armstrong, who he has now outlived for a number of decades. He has survived eighteen of our forty-four presidents. But maybe the best gauge of how long he has lived and how far we have come is to remember how, in 1896, only fifteen years before Ferbos was born, the Supreme Court upheld "separate but equal" when it mandated that Homer Plessy, also a Seventh Ward Creole, ride only in segregated streetcars. Over a hundred years later, Ferbos had lived long enough to receive a one hundredth-birthday letter from a black president. "Separate but equal" is a thing of the past, but the musical contributions of Lionel Ferbos are still very much in the present.

FRANKIE FORD

Frankie Ford's home in Gretna, Louisiana, across the river from New Orleans, has much the same rock and roll, 1950s vibe as Graceland. Photographs of musical legends and memorabilia of Ford's lengthy, international career cover every inch of the walls. A huge piano dominates the living room. The furniture has a retro, 1950s look, suggesting that Ford and Elvis had more in common than just their music. During our conversation, XM radio's 1950s station plays appropriately in the background.

A gracious and charming host, Ford is comfortable in the house he built in 1960 and where he has lived ever since. He remains a familiar figure around town, easily recognizable in his Lincoln Town Car with the "Ooh-Wee" vanity license plate.

Born in 1940, Ford, the adopted son of an Italian couple, grew up in Gretna. He appeared on-stage by age five and at thirteen earned his first money singing on the *Ted Mack Amateur Hour*. The city's thriving R&B scene deeply influenced him; "I used to sneak into the Joy Lounge to listen to Sugar Boy Crawford and Frogman Henry." He explains, "You know, back then, we didn't worry much about race and music. We played together and learned from each other."

Ford hit it big in 1958 when he recorded "Sea Cruise" in Cosimo Matassa's legendary New Orleans studio. Ford sang the lyrics over Huey "Piano" Smith's backing track. *Rolling Stone* called Ford's signature song "the finest example of pure-stomping New Orleans rock ever made." Ford's ensuing popularity led to fourteen appearances on *American Bandstand*. He went on to play venues such as the Hollywood Bowl, Royal Albert Hall, and the Lincoln Center, never losing his enthusiasm, explaining, "I haven't had a real job my whole life."

Ford is married to Barbara, the piano player at Pat O'Brien's in the Quarter since 1967. In 2009, the flamboyant couple was the King and Queen of the irreverent Krewe du Vieux—they still enthusiastically participate in the unique rituals of their hometown.

PETE FOUNTAIN

Performing or not, few New Orleans musicians are more closely associated with the streets of the French Quarter than jazz clarinetist Pete Fountain. It is where he played as a kid and listened to music, where he had his club for many years, and where he caroused with his close friend, Al Hirt, shutting down more than their fair share of Bourbon Street bistros. And it is where Fountain has chosen to be interviewed and photographed, in Pirate's Alley right behind St. Louis Cathedral.

It is a beautiful fall day. The longtime Archbishop of New Orleans, Philip Hannan, has just died and the streets around the cathedral are blocked in preparation for the Archbishop's funeral. Using a cane as a result of recent health problems, Fountain approaches a police barricade, an impish gleam still in his eyes, notwithstanding his age. He holds his clarinet. The police immediately recognize this denizen of the Quarter and wave him right through.

Fountain was born in 1930 as Peter LaFontaine Jr. and grew up in Mid-City. A sickly child, he took up the clarinet when he was nine after his doctor suggested it might improve his lung strength. He would listen outside to clubs on Bourbon Street, hiding behind trash containers and absorbing the rhythms of the city's jazz legends. Influenced by George Lewis, Irving Fazola, and Benny Goodman, he took a little from each to create his own signature sound. After high school in 1950, he went straight to Bourbon Street to form the Basin Street Six with whom he made his first recordings.

For a while, Fountain struggled financially. To supplement their incomes, Fountain and Al Hirt worked for a pest-control company, an unlikely experiment that lasted only two months. Not long after, Fountain got his big break from a call from Lawrence Welk. He moved to California only to return to New Orleans in 1959, so his three kids could "grow up like I did." Running nightclubs, recording fifty-six albums (and a featured performer on another forty-four), Fountain became one of the most recognizable jazz artists in the world. He appeared on the *Tonight Show* fifty-nine times, played for four different presidents, and entertained Pope John Paul II at a papal mass in 1987.

Fountain accomplished all of this while keeping his uniquely New Orleans ability to enjoy a good time. Founder of the Half-Fast Walking Club, a marching krewe (originally named the Half-Assed Walking Club, which proved objectionable to more straight-laced parade organizers), Fountain still makes his way every Mardi Gras morning from Commander's Palace to the Quarter, now riding in a float instead of walking. And he still provides memorable moments. When asked for a song that Archbishop Hannan might have enjoyed, Fountain plays "Do You Know What it Means to Miss New Orleans?" As the notes slowly reverberate across Jackson Square, Fountain finishes and smiles. He reflects, "Only in this city could a saloon player from the Quarter be an Archbishop's pal. Isn't that wonderful?"

HELEN GILLET

Musicians' Village in the Ninth Ward is home to all kinds of musicians finding residential refuge post-Katrina. Helen Gillet may be the only one who is a classically trained cellist and is probably the only one born in Belgium and raised in Singapore. Then again, it is New Orleans, so even that may not be a safe bet.

Gillet's home is full of travel cases and musical instruments, including a piano in the living room. It gives physical reminder to Gillet's heavy touring schedule, much of it international, and to her willingness to experiment with forms of music well beyond her original, classical training. The furnishings are personal and eclectic, reflecting her improvisational and creative style.

Gillet and her mother moved to Chicago from Singapore when she was twelve. There, she took up the cello and continued to play classically at college in Wisconsin. But she wanted "more musical freedom, something different, something impromptu." That kind of thinking leads you straight to New Orleans. She moved here in 2003, when she was twenty-three, and felt right at home: "The weather reminded me of Singapore. I loved the French influence. The musicians were so welcoming." While getting her masters in classical cello at Loyola and playing wedding gigs around town, she got her big break when bassist James Singleton hired her for a string quartet.

Gillet expanded her musical horizons, embracing jazz, soul, funk, and a healthy dose of French chansons. She played with the likes of Johnny Vidacovich and the New Orleans Bingo! Show, the latter indulging her fondness for masking, costumes, and occasionally bizarre finery. She was among the early returners after Katrina, busking Jackson Square at Christmas to earn rent money. After she was featured on the cover of *Offbeat*'s 2010 Mardi Gras issue, she gained confidence and notoriety and enjoyed even greater success, both locally and internationally.

Thoughtful and playful, Gillet enjoys her Musicians' Village neighbors such as Smokey Johnson, legendary drummer for Fats Domino and a source of constant encouragement. As a young woman playing a classical instrument, she was at first unsure of how the city's musicians would react to her. Johnson's support has been typical: "The older musicians especially have been very respectful. But that's New Orleans. Somehow this city just ties it all together, for me personally and musically."

VICTOR GOINES

As much educator as musician, jazz saxophonist and clarinetist Victor Goines moves comfortably through the halls of St. Augustine High School, his alma mater in New Orleans's Seventh Ward. He exchanges greetings with students and faculty alike, an obviously familiar member of the tight and extremely loyal "St. Aug" family. He walks into classrooms where he once was a student and later returned to teach math.

The all-boys school is a pristine oasis in a still-recovering neighborhood. Goines remembers his teachers, the same instructors who taught him math and English and also polished his skills on the horn. They were building on what the nuns in earlier grades had already started, a parochial education that combined discipline and music and that Goines readily concedes has provided the foundation for his later successes.

One of five children growing up in the Eighth Ward, Goines began playing the clarinet at age eight ("I wanted to play drums, but my mother said, 'Five kids, no drums,'") using its breathing techniques to help with his asthma. Carl Blouin Sr. introduced him to the saxophone at St. Augustine. Goines played in all-state ensembles with both Wynton and Branford Marsalis. He went to Loyola and eventually studied with Ellis Marsalis, who asked Goines to play the sax in his quartet. When Marsalis left New Orleans to teach in Richmond, Goines followed and earned a masters in music from Virginia Commonwealth in 1990.

Goines shuffled back and forth between New York and New Orleans for a few years, playing on Broadway, teaching at the University of New Orleans, and playing with Lionel Hampton, Dizzy Gillespie, and others. In 1993, his old friend Wynton asked him to join the Wynton Marsalis Septet and Jazz at the Lincoln Center Orchestra. He has twenty-one releases to his playing credit, with seven as lead, and more than fifty original compositional works. For seven years, Goines was artistic director of the Juilliard School jazz program and a faculty member teaching saxophone and clarinet. His educational resume is extraordinary, having served on the faculties of Florida A&M, UNO, Loyola, and Xavier universities. Goines is now Director of Jazz Studies and Professor of Music at Northwestern University's Bienen School of Music.

The students at St. Augustine reflect its emphasis on discipline and walking respectfully through the halls in uniform. The well-mannered and focused Goines absorbed its lessons well. And he feels an obligation to give back, to pay homage to his teachers: "Mr. Winchester, Mr. Hampton, Mr. Blouin, Mr. Richardson, to the nuns, to Ellis Marsalis." Goines remembers them each with fondness and respect, saying, "I am just part of a long line in this city. I have an obligation to pass it on, performing and especially teaching."

DONALD HARRISON JR.

*L*ocated on Jefferson Street in Uptown, Isidore Newman School has educated scores of prominent New Orleanians for more than a century. Its graduates include Rhodes Scholars, award-winning authors, and Super Bowl quarterbacks. It is here that jazz saxophonist Donald Harrison Jr. chose to be photographed. Harrison teaches at the New Jazz School, a Newman summer program, where he works with dozens of young musicians, tutoring them in the musical craft of their city.

As Harrison chats with his visitors, his students continue to practice independently in the background, preparing for the concert that will eventually conclude the program. To a lesser ear, the competing horns can sound like a jazz cacophony, but not to the teacher. The polite and soft-spoken Harrison suddenly stops the interview, picking out a few notes, and asks, "Did you hear that? That's what I'm looking for. They like what they are playing. That's good."

That Harrison's influence would extend into the halls of an Uptown private school is not surprising. He has long transcended musical boundaries. Harrison is the son of a legendary Mardi Gras Indian chief, who encouraged Harrison to take up the saxophone when he was sixteen ("he challenged me

to play Charlie Parker, what he called real music"). Trained by some of the city's best musicians, such as Alvin Batiste, Kid Jordan, and Ellis Marsalis, he eventually ended up in New York City. He spent twenty years there playing modern jazz with the likes of Roy Haynes, Art Blakely, and Miles Davis.

But the lure of his hometown remained strong, and in 2001, Harrison returned. "I love this place: its buildings, its parrots, its shrimp and oyster po' boys, the way we talk to each other in the street. I have to have it." Called a "one man Jazz Fest" by the *Times-Picayune,* the disciplined Harrison has an extraordinary musical versatility and an expansive range, which includes traditional jazz, classical, be-bop, and hip-hop. Now the chief of his own tribe, the Congo Nation, Harrison freely mixes Mardi Gras Indian rhythms into his performances and compositions.

Harrison is an enthusiastic teacher. He speaks proudly of his nephew, Christian Scott, also on the faculty of the New Jazz School. Especially mindful of the fragility of the city's musical tradition, he is determined to pass it on. "New Orleans and its music constitute the soul of America. Katrina tested that soul. Our roots run deep, but they still have to be nourished, or we could lose everything."

CLARENCE "FROGMAN" HENRY

Across the river from downtown New Orleans, Frogman Henry lives in the city's Algiers neighborhood, his home since 1948. Much of his extended family still lives nearby. With two large concrete frogs adorning the front entrance of his comfortable brick home, Henry is not especially hard to find. The legendary R&B singer chose to be photographed there, surrounded by hundreds of stuffed, plastic, and rubber frogs of all shapes and sizes, given to him by fans since 1957. Frogs are everywhere: suspended from the ceiling, on Henry's piano, and next to the many photographs chronicling Frogman's long and successful career.

Though battling health issues and using a walker and an occasional wheelchair, Frogman remains an extremely popular performer in his hometown, playing Jazz Fest and appearing on WWOZ radio. Warm and generous, Frogman even included the interviewer on his Christmas card list. His signature song, "Ain't Got No Home," contradicts the reality of his close ties to his family and to New Orleans and its music community.

A friend and contemporary of Fats Domino, Professor Longhair, and Allen Toussaint, Henry played trombone and piano in a high school band, the Toppers, with Bobby Mitchell ("I'm Gonna Be a Wheel Someday"). Mitchell fired Henry when Henry failed to show up one night because "I was getting married." Henry continued to play at clubs, especially on the West Bank. It was at the Joy Lounge one late evening when the crowd refused to leave and an exhausted Henry howled "Oooh oh oh oh" and lamented in his husky voice that the crowd "ain't got no home." Henry issued the song as the B-side to *Troubles Troubles,* but New Orleans DJ Poppa Stoppa gave it extended play in response to listeners asking for "that frog song." An unforgettable identity was born when Poppa Stoppa told the gravelly-voiced Henry that he would be "Frogman" from then on. Henry went on to become a fixture in Bourbon Street clubs for more than twenty years.

Frogman attracted the admiration of the Beatles, opening for the Fab Four eighteen times on their first American tour. He became a lifelong friend of Paul McCartney, "just a wonderful guy who could really take my money playing dice."

An enthusiastic proponent of the institution of marriage, at the time of this interview, Frogman had been married eight times and had ten children, seventeen grandchildren, and fifteen great-grandchildren. He keeps a family tree sketched on an envelope in his den, explaining, "It's really the only way I can keep track of everybody's names."

BEN JAFFE

When choosing a place for his photograph, bass and tuba player Ben Jaffe opted for Preservation Hall, the iconic French Quarter traditional-jazz venue where Jaffe, the son of the Hall's cofounders Allan and Sandra Jaffe and a member of the Preservation Hall Jazz Band, regularly performs. Jaffe makes this call because in addition to being his stage, the Hall has always been his home.

Preservation Hall had been open ten years by the time Jaffe was born in 1971. The courtyard where he is seen here became his home, his playground, his daycare center, and his classroom. In the courtyard, his were no ordinary babysitters and teachers—they were jazz legends such as Willie and Percy Humphrey, Sweet Emma Barrett, Lionel Ferbos, and Lars Edegran. Exposure like that pretty much foreordains a career; as Jaffe says, "By the time I was six, I knew I was going to be a musician."

Jaffe was playing bass in the school band the next year. The band's director was Walter Payton, father of trumpeter Nicholas Payton. Jaffe attended the New Orleans Center for Creative Arts and experienced his only time of "musical rebellion" when he experimented with modern jazz under the tutelage of Ellis Marsalis. After the premature death of his father and his graduation from Oberlin College in 1993, Jaffe returned to New Orleans. He joined the Preservation Hall Jazz Band as its bassist, eventually assuming the role as the Hall's director. He began playing the tuba and ended up teaching back at NOCCA.

Jaffe is a serious student of the city's musical history. He enjoys tracing its roots by listening to Alan Lomax field recordings and West African music and by traveling to Brazil to "appreciate where all this came from and what we are connected to." With his wife, he founded the New Orleans Musician Hurricane Relief Fund and has filmed several documentaries that celebrate the city's musical traditions.

Most of all, the soft-spoken Jaffe believes that his connection to the Hall imposes upon him an "intense responsibility to the city, its music, its African-American community, which is the heart of our culture." Inviting acts such as U2's the Edge and the New Orleans Bingo! Show into the Hall, he strives to continue to make the old space relevant while protecting ("I like that word better than preserving") its jazz traditions. Sometimes he wishes that more locals partook of the Hall's pleasures, but that hardly diminishes its status as his home, where he pays homage to his parents' dream and to the city they loved.

CONNIE JONES

Everything about jazz trumpet and cornet player Connie Jones is comfortable: his personality, his neat home near City Park, and his relationship with his wife, Elaine ("after you guys leave, I am going to get Connie to mow the yard"). In many ways, Jones is a musician's musician; he remains as unpretentious as the traditional jazz he plays, a link to the city's musical past.

Jones's home is full of reminders of all of his years in music. He and Elaine proudly show their visitors around, telling stories about the pictures of Jones's many bands, highlighting the French Quarter Fest 2011 poster that featured Jones and his good friends Pete Fountain and Tim Laughlin.

Jones started in plastics, his first instrument a plastic bugle he picked up as a ten-year-old in military school. He soon received an actual cornet as a birthday gift and worked his way into the school band. By eighteen, he was playing traditional jazz on Bourbon Street, where he met clarinetist Fountain. The two became original members of the Basin Street Six. His relationship with Fountain has endured, with Pete serving as Jones's best man and with Jones doing several stints in Fountain's bands.

Jones left music in the late 1950s to run his own gas station on Airline Highway in New Orleans. The high risks of that business ("I actually got held up twice in the same night") and the low rewards ("I actually had to go back to music to make money") led him to New York, where he joined the band of legendary trombonist Jack Teagarden until Teagarden's death in 1966. He eventually returned to his hometown, played lead trumpet for Fountain and then for the Dukes of Dixieland, and headlined his own band at the Blue Angel nightclub on Bourbon Street. Jones continues to play around town, often with fellow tradition-bearers such as Laughlin and Tom McDermott. He deeply values the musical community, saying, "When I was growing up, everybody helped you, you just asked. That hasn't changed much."

Jones's home was flooded by Hurricane Katrina, which destroyed much of his considerable sheet music collection. When he and Elaine returned, they found only one surviving score that now hangs prominently on their living room wall—Hurricane Rag.

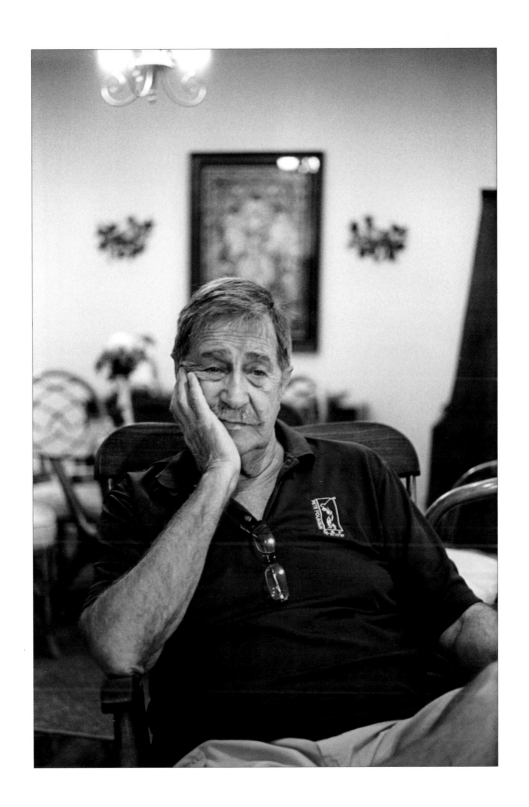

LITTLE FREDDIE KING

The phone rings in the Musicians' Village home of blues guitarist Little Freddie King. But King at first can't find it. It's buried somewhere under a pile of papers on his coffee table, letters from fans, requests for him to perform, and notes and programs, all evidence of the continuing popularity of one of the city's great gutbucket blues guitarists.

King's home pays homage to his career, with photos and posters of his performances and snippets of interviews everywhere. A voodoo stick is propped in the corner. Easy-going with an infectious laugh, he relaxes on his sofa with one of his several guitars right next to him, ever the bluesman even when not performing.

King literally rode the rails to New Orleans from his McComb, Mississippi, home. Born Fread Martin, he grew up around the blues watching his father, a cousin of Lightnin' Hopkins, play guitar and listening to Muddy Waters. Not allowed to play his father's guitar ("tried once and got worse whuppin' I ever had"), he fashioned his first instrument out of a cigar box and horse hair. After a 1954 visit to New Orleans, the lure of the big city proved too strong. Back home in Mississippi, the fourteen-year-old jumped a freight train and hung on for dear life to the door of an open box car, "floppin' around in the wind for near half a mile." His arrival in the city was just as perilous—he jumped off the still-moving train and "tore my skin, my pants, my shirt. Didn't jump no more trains." He went looking for his sister's house, caught the eye of a suspicious cop, and was saved from arrest by the intervention of a local gas station owner.

King went to work at the gas station, but he was determined to learn guitar. He bought his first one from Sears (he eventually would own dozens, most destroyed by Katrina) and tried to figure out how to play. "Radio was no help," he claims. "They would run me off Bourbon Street, so I bought a record player and slowed all the forty-fives down to thirty-three and one-third. That worked." King loved South Louisiana blues, the music of Polka Dot Slim and Boogie Jack. Influenced by famed Chicago blues guitarist Freddie King, Little Freddie took his name diminutively and had the chance to play "bass with him, but only once." Since his rocky arrival, King has come a long way—touring with Bo Diddley, playing with James Booker, and headlining clubs such as BJ's Lounge in the Lower Ninth, all with a trademark flamboyant and hard-driving style.

King still has eight guitars left in his home. He also is proud of his bicycle, "my two-wheeled Cadillac, I ride it every day." As a means of transportation for Little Freddie, evidently it beats the train.

TIM LAUGHLIN

Very few addresses in New Orleans more befit a dedicated preservationist of the city's musical and architectural traditions than one on Royal Street in the French Quarter. That is where jazz clarinetist Tim Laughlin lives, in a second-story home built in 1811 for a French attorney and meticulously restored by Laughlin and his wife after they bought it in 2008.

Laughlin's decorations reflect his respect for tradition—a large grand piano in a double parlor overlooking Royal, a lamp made from his first clarinet, and dozens of photographs and posters of young and old jazz musicians. Laughlin loves standing on the balcony and watching parades such as Krewe du Vieux. He frequently invites his many friends in the local music community to his home to jam with the sounds of music cascading out of the floor-to-ceiling windows into the Quarter below.

Laughlin grew up in the Gentilly neighborhood and attended high school at Holy Cross in the Ninth Ward. A longtime fan of Mardi Gras, he first was paid to play while riding on a Pegasus float when he was fifteen. Two years later, he met the legendary Pete Fountain, who remains his mentor and close friend. Both Fountain and Laughlin consider themselves heirs to the influential but short-lived jazz clarinet tradition of New Orleans's Irving Fazola, who died in 1949 at age thirty-six. After Katrina destroyed many of his instruments in his Lakeview home, Fountain gave Laughlin "Old Betsy," one of his favorite clarinets with a mouthpiece that once belonged to Fazola.

Laughlin plays Old Betsy in his many shows around town in clubs such as the Palm Court Jazz Café, the Bombay Club, Fritzel's European Jazz Pub, and the Roosevelt Blue Room, which he reopened with Fountain in 2009. He continues to compose and play with other traditionalists such as Tom McDermott and Connie Jones. He showed his passion for New Orleans and traditional jazz ("I really don't ever want to live anywhere else") when, after the storm, he toured Peru, Canada, and Mexico for the United States Department of State to raise money to buy instruments for the New Orleans Center for Creative Arts.

Laughlin is genial, almost but not quite shy, with a humorous, playful side. He is proud of the bumper sticker he claims to have created: "New Orleans, we put the fun in funeral." He carries his clarinet in a doctor's bag and likes his five-toed Vibram shoes just because "they are weird." And he still is invested in Mardi Gras, riding every Fat Tuesday morning with Pete Fountain on the first float of the Half-Fast Walking Club.

DELFEAYO MARSALIS

In his Uptown home, jazz trombonist and producer Delfeayo Marsalis meticulously prepares a cup of tea in his well-ordered kitchen. He knows his teas and has a large collection of teapots collected during his many tours, both domestic and international. Hot water is always at the ready, he says, because "Like the Japanese, I want to be able to pour a cup of tea whenever I want." It seems a long way from the somewhat more dissolute lifestyle of one of his musical heroes, Miles Davis.

But Delfeayo is a Marsalis, the fourth-oldest son of that famously-disciplined musical family. He is very much at ease, animated and friendly. Every bit the Marsalis, he laughs about his father's "old school" approach to raising six sons and about big brothers Branford and Wynton "feeling like they had to act the part." Like other family members, he is very interested in jazz history and owns an extensive music collection of tapes and CDs neatly stored in elegant, custom-made shelving.

Ellis Marsalis put a premium on educating his sons. Delfeayo was no exception, attending NOCCA, training at Tanglewood, graduating from Berklee College of Music, and obtaining a masters from Louisville. Inspired by J. J. Johnson and others, Marsalis took up the trombone when he was thirteen. After finishing school, he toured with jazz legends such as Art Blakely, Elvin Jones, Max Roach, and Absullah Ibrahim. He has released a number of albums as a band leader, including *Such Sweet Thunder* in 2011, an ambitious project that reinterprets the work of Duke Ellington and Billy Strayhorn to reflect more modern sensibilities.

Delfeayo is also a talented producer with more than one hundred recordings, including work for Harry Connick Jr., Terence Blanchard, Spike Lee, the Preservation Hall Jazz Band, and his father and brothers. Even these talents found their inspiration from the family circle, as Branford taught Delfeayo in the fifth grade how to create a feedback loop on a reel to reel machine and as Wynton challenged him in the seventh grade to produce a demo tape with the same quality as a good classical studio recording.

Delfeayo recognizes his place in the pantheon of New Orleans musicians. Like the rest of his family, he is sensitive to his debt to those who have come before and to his obligations to those who will follow. He understands the importance of education in preserving and progressing the city's musical traditions. Initially, he considered having his photo taken at Dillard University, where he teaches. In 2000, he helped found the Uptown Music Theater, which uses music and theater to empower children to make good choices within the constructs of the city's great cultural traditions. If anyone is qualified to impart these lessons, it is a Marsalis.

ELLIS MARSALIS

When jazz pianist Ellis Marsalis is not performing, he is teaching—through his word, through his deed, through his style, through his passion. Education is the great obsession that has allowed him to become the revered patriarch of one of New Orleans's most talented and well-known musical families. Photographed on the front porch of the quiet Carrollton home, where he has lived with his wife Dolores since 1975 (except for a three-year stint teaching in Richmond), Marsalis turns practically every conversation back around to education, arguing that even Louis Armstrong probably learned more music from teachers than he ever did in a brothel.

Education and the attendant need for discipline would seem a pre-requisite for raising six sons. Branford, Wynton, Delfeayo, and Jason have all carved out unique, highly personal musical niches, with their successes founded on training "with great teachers and other great students," which their father demanded. When Branford and his friend Harry Connick Jr. established Musicians' Village post-Katrina, it was only natural that they would name the Village's education and performance venue the Ellis Marsalis Center for Music.

Born in 1934, Ellis grew up in the Gert Town neighborhood of New Orleans. Unlike many of his contemporaries, he has no particular recollection of hearing music in the streets and no particular early musical influences other than Dizzy Gillespie. To Marsalis, it was less about the vernacular of the streets and more about what he could learn in the classroom. He played the clarinet and tenor sax as a teenager, switching to the piano after graduating from Dillard University with a degree in music education. He free-lanced around town, accompanying Al Hirt and playing in the Storyville Jazz Band.

But mostly Marsalis was teaching, first as an adjunct jazz instructor at Xavier University. After earning a masters degree in music education at Loyola, he was hired as the head of the music department at the New Orleans Center for Creative Arts (NOCCA). There, he mentored the new generation of jazz artists: musicians such as Donald Harrison Jr., Terence Blanchard, Harry Connick Jr., Nicholas Payton, and Kent and Marlon Jordan. After three years in Richmond teaching at Virginia Commonwealth University, he returned to New Orleans in 1989 to accept a position as the head of the Jazz Studies Program at the University of New Orleans, where he remained for twelve years. By the 1980s, his recording career blossomed, and he became a popular Frenchman Street performer with a regular Friday-night gig at Snug Harbor.

During his interview, the modest and gracious Marsalis pulls out a copy of Al Kennedy's book *Chord Changes on the Chalkboard: How Public School Teachers Shaped Jazz and the Music of New Orleans*. Written by one of his UNO graduate students, it is one of Marsalis's favorite books, an affirmation of his belief (and of his life) that musical success comes best from lessons well taught.

JASON MARSALIS

When you are a Marsalis, a member of one of the first families of New Orleans jazz, it may be that you are never not performing. The family's stature and reputation ensures as much. Thus, when it came time for the youngest family member, percussionist Jason Marsalis, to choose a spot for his photograph, he selected the courtyard of a Bourbon Street club at which he frequently performs, close but not actually on the stage.

It is a languid July day, well over ninety degrees in heat, and humid like only New Orleans can be in the summer. But the goateed, bespectacled, and skinny Marsalis looks the part of a cool jazz drummer, the only heat emitted when he passionately discusses jazz history and how "too many younger musicians don't know the songs, don't know their history." This is a Marsalis family refrain, and the youngest brother has fully absorbed the message.

Jason started playing drums when he was three, and later took up the violin, but "by the time I was twelve, I realized I was a percussionist." That year, he played his first gig with his father, Ellis; at age fourteen, he appeared on one of Ellis's CDs; and then he studied classical percussion at Loyola. He further honed his skills by playing with artists such as Harold Battiste and Roland Guerin. His career gained traction in the late 1990s with the release of his first CD in 1998 and his successful participation in the Latin fusion band Los Hombres Calientes.

In the early part of the 2000s, Marsalis affiliated himself with preeminent jazz pianist, Marcus Roberts, and formed his own quintet. By the end of the decade, he began to experiment with the vibraphone, winning praise from Ben Ratliff of the *New York Times* such as, "an excellent musician trying out something risky without embarrassment." Both on the drums and vibraphone, Marsalis has a distinctive visual style, his head bobbing in an exaggerated fashion as he fulfills what he calls the percussionist's role of "keeping the groove."

Jason has been called by his older brothers and by others as the most talented member of the family. As the youngest, he has had many mentors and plenty of opportunities to learn from the best. But he claims he has never felt any "Marsalis expectations." He explains, "Family is family. I make my own expectations. And I believe in what I am doing." And with that, Marsalis strolls out of the courtyard and back on to Bourbon Street, someone comfortable in his own (very cool) skin.

THREE MASAKOWSKIS

What was going to be a session with jazz guitarist Steve Masakowski became a lot more when we arrived at his Uptown home. Like many New Orleans families, there is more than one musical Masakowski. His wife, classical pianist Ulrike, and daughter, jazz singer Sasha, were both in the living room, giving us a rare opportunity to chat with all of them. When not performing, the three Masakowskis are obviously most relaxed and at ease with family: completing each other's sentences, laughing about their inability to remember their anniversary, and disagreeing about how Steve and Ulrike met (it was either at the club Tyler's or at Loyola, but in any event it was in New Orleans).

Steve was raised in Uptown, first hearing jazz on his front porch, where he spent a lot of time given his house's lack of air conditioning (a common theme in interviews with musicians of a certain age, leading to the question of whether there would have been any jazz if AC had come along one hundred years earlier). Inspired by the Beatles, the young guitar player ultimately went in a different direction, graduating from the Berklee School of Music and launching a career as one of jazz's most creative improvisers. He spent time in New York and recorded for famed label Blue Note Records, but moved back to New Orleans where he also created a distinguished career as an educator, holding an endowed chair in jazz studies at the University of New Orleans. A member of the Astral Project, Masakowski has played with "pretty much every musician in town." He says, "That is what I love about this place—no cliques like in New York. Here the musicians are always willing to try different stuff."

His wife, Ulrike, is German and classically trained from childhood. Influenced by an interview with Fats Domino, she came to New Orleans because of its music. She continued her career as a concert pianist but sought to absorb the style of her adopted hometown, taking lessons from Dr. John and Eddie Bo. Also an educator, she is the author of *Reeka Rules*, a piano-method course.

Daughter Sasha is an emerging star in jazz singing (says Steve, "People always ask me if I am related to Sasha, no one ever asks her if she is related to me.") A musical theater graduate from NOCCA, she prefers the more improvisational style of jazz. She went to the Rotterdam Conservatory of Music and studied in her dad's program at UNO. Sasha has the advantage of youthful energy: she played in China for five months, fronts for two bands, and plays in two others.

There is yet more talent in the Masakowski family. Brother Martin, an acoustic bassist, was not there that day because he was touring in Europe. But the Masakowskis stick together. Go to a Jazz Fest session expecting to see one of them, and you are likely to get any or all of them, keeping the New Orleans tradition of family-style music alive.

TOM McDERMOTT

*I*t takes a certain laid-back personality to welcome visitors to your Mid-City home wearing nothing but shorts, a paint-splattered t-shirt, and swim goggles. But it makes perfect sense when you consider the scorching September heat and the need to paint the front porch of the house where you have lived since 1997 (the swim goggles might still be a mystery). And it also is just the affable personality of jazz pianist Tom McDermott.

After inviting his visitors in, McDermott showers and changes. Before beginning our session, he further surprises us, exclaiming "You gotta see this." He goes to his closest and pulls out a seersucker suit. "This belonged to Walker Percy." A friend to whom McDermott was teaching the piano had given him the suit of the famous New Orleans novelist as a gift. There are all sorts of ways to get paid in this town.

McDermott is a native of St. Louis, Missouri, and his soft-spoken and thoughtful style at first might seem more suggestive of the Midwest than of his adopted home of New Orleans. McDermott began playing the piano at age six, fell in love with ragtime, and had his first gig at Shakey's Pizza. After getting a masters at Washington University of St. Louis, McDermott free-lanced as a music critic for a St. Louis paper. He had visited New Orleans as a teenager, and by the early 1980s, his affection for James Booker and the city's unbelievably rich piano tradition ("Jelly Roll, Fats, Booker, Butler, Toussaint, Cleary, Dr. John, I mean, come on") convinced him to move south.

McDermott played the 1984 World's Fair, steamboats, and inevitably Bourbon Street. "I worked the midnight-to-5 A.M. shift at a club that had recently been a whorehouse," he says. "Lots of people who came in didn't know about the change. Made for an exotic introduction to New Orleans." He played with the Dukes of Dixieland and helped start the New Orleans Nightcrawlers, an innovative brass band. But he was interested in expanding his musical horizons. He first went to Brazil in 1989 and, beginning in 2000, made another fourteen trips there, exploring that country's traditions and their similarities to those of New Orleans. He is especially fascinated by Brazilian *choro,* which merges European harmonies with African rhythms.

McDermott's living room is crowded with hundreds of books and thousands of albums. It is dominated by a piano. A talented composer, McDermott sits down and rips off one of his original choro compositions by ear, without wearing the swim goggles.

PHILIP MELANCON

*R*elaxing in the Neutral Ground, the Uptown coffee shop he used to own as an "involuntary non-profit," cabaret singer Philip Melancon is a long way from the classrooms of Jefferson Parish, where he taught for twenty years before deciding to earn his living as a musician. He provided a similar mentoring experience at the Neutral Ground, showcasing the talents of local musicians for tips only, with a sharp sense of humor and plenty of colorful stories.

Wearing a shirt he purchased for $5 right off of the back of Alien, a Neutral Ground-regular, the golfing Melancon is especially proud of the eighteenth-hole tee-marker he uses as a table. He claims that the marker mysteriously showed up in the coffee shop the night the old City Park South golf course closed in 2005.

Born in the Gert Town neighborhood of New Orleans, Melancon received his first guitar from his Uncle Mickey, whose own repertoire was limited to "Blue Moon," sung loudly and often at family gatherings. Perhaps as a result, Melancon decided to go into teaching instead of music, never missing a day in the classroom for two decades. But as a twelve-year-old, he composed a song, "Millie the Cow." Twenty-five years late, the local children's TV show, *Popeye and Pals*, needed a "cow song" (a fortuitous request in a city where songs about saints abound, but bovine music is in comparatively short supply). Melancon let them use "Millie the Cow."

Melancon decided to try a living in music before "it became too late to catch the streetcar." He taught himself the piano by ear and became a regular on the cabaret circuit, playing familiar venues such as the Pontchartrain and Columns Hotels. When Katrina hit, Melancon stayed in town. When soldiers heard him through the open windows playing his piano in his apartment, they moved the piano to Audubon Park, and Melancon played the first concert in the city after the storm. He calls it "my own little USO tour."

Melancon is self-deprecating, saying, "I am just a bar fly with a portfolio." But the *New York Times* sees it somewhat differently, admiring Melancon's style and a voice "marinated in the saloons of New Orleans," with a touch of caffeine on the side.

AMASA MILLER

On his raised double in the shadow of Notre Dame Seminary near the intersection of Carrollton and Earhart, pianist Amasa Miller is juicing fruits and vegetables. This is not typical New Orleans cuisine but maybe more the style of the "former hippie" that Miller claims to be. Given Miller's role since the 1980s as one of the most active sidemen in the city, often playing three hundred gigs per year ("one Jazz Fest, I played twenty-six gigs in ten days"), healthy eating would seem to be a prerequisite.

Signs of Miller's hands-on talent are everywhere. One room at a time, he is remodeling his home, which flooded after Katrina. He is combining rooms, the interior contrasting with the exterior in stark and appealing fashion. Scattered around are several instruments he is repairing and restringing for upcoming gigs.

A self-described "workaday musician," Miller is from Montclair, New Jersey, where his 1950s "Beaver Cleaver" lifestyle evolved into a classic 1960s journey through Antioch College, the Ivy League, draft issues, migrant farms, the streets of Paris, and then a Belgian commune (that pretty much sums up the sixties as a whole). Miller supported himself with music: the ukulele, the guitar, and ultimately a jug band. After returning to the States, he played piano in a country-swing band in New England and moved to New Orleans in 1981 after his wife tired of cold winters.

Miller immediately became obsessed with James Booker, whose performances he tried to never miss: "With all his problems, Booker never played a wrong note . . . was a genius but only really sane when he was playing." Miller's first local gig was with John Mooney at the Maple Leaf Bar. He started playing piano solo at Molly Monahan's and then joined up with the Pfister Sisters in 1981, which resulted in one of the longest-running gigs in New Orleans. He didn't stop there—shortly thereafter he began backing Charmaine Neville, a thirty-year gig, with the last twenty taking place at Snug Harbor for their legendary Monday-night show. With his self-effacing style, Miller got plenty of sideman opportunities, working with Little Queenie, Aaron Neville, and others in most of the city's many venues.

Miller says that gigs have slowed some in recent years: "9/11, the storm, the economy, the oil spill, it's been sort of a rough decade." But despite his claim that he is "an alien, just a white guy from New Jersey," Miller remains an important part of the city's musical scene, someone who is willing to make his living as a sideman while displaying the talents of a lead.

FRANK MINYARD

*L*ike so many others, Frank Minyard was forever changed by Katrina. His case is particularly astute since he is the city's coroner, charged with chronicling the terrible loss of human life after the levees broke. The past few years have not been easy. In April 2011, his offices caught fire. When photographed, he worked in sparsely furnished, temporary offices on Rampart Street, with few signs of the colorful career of the longest serving elected official in the history of New Orleans.

As coroner, Minyard memorably captures the connection between the city's music and its fascination with death. A former obstetrician, Minyard has been coroner since the mid-seventies. But he also is a musician, a trumpeter whose dedication to the city's legacy of good times mixed with good music is the stuff of legend.

Raised in Gentilly, Minyard learned to play the trumpet by ear, encouraged by his ragtime piano-playing mother. But when he went to high school at Holy Cross, he gave up music. He went to college and medical school at LSU and completed his residency at the city's famed Charity Hospital. He opened a medical practice that prospered and by the late 1960s found himself thoroughly enjoying the city's many pleasures. He was looking for something more, however, and after several forays into public service, he was elected coroner in 1973, the same year that Harry Connick Sr. won his first term as DA.

As of 2012, Minyard has been reelected nine times.

It was not until he was forty that Minyard picked his horn back up. Appearing on a New Orleans radio talk-show, he fielded a call from his mother who told him she was having his old trumpet re-furbished. Unaware that Minyard had once played, host Keith Rush invited him back to perform. His return was less than an unqualified success; callers such as friend Pete Fountain strongly encouraged him to keep his day job. But he stuck with it and got better under the tutelage of musicians such as Milton Batiste and the Olympia Brass Band. He played gigs all over town with friends such as the Connicks Sr. and Jr. Given his profession, he always knew when second line funerals would take place and how to get a spot in the parade.

Minyard has made a tangible commitment to the city's musicians. As founder and president of Jazz Roots, which has raised over $800,000 through the years, Minyard claims never to have met a musician he didn't like. But Katrina has taken a huge toll on the gregarious Minyard, both personally and professionally. Since the storm, he has considered public music performances inappropriate, saying, "Katrina took my joy, my soul, my music." Recently remarried and reinvigorated, Minyard has picked up his horn again. As the city heals, he may yet contribute to the sounds of the streets he has loved for so long.

J MONQUE'D

Sitting on J Monque'D's front porch on a steamy summer day with the Mississippi River just a few blocks away is the best way to listen to the many stories of this gregarious blues harmonica-player. When it gets hot and humid in New Orleans, time slows down. It's time in which you can fully appreciate the life and legends of J.

The sterility of air-conditioning would not do justice to the colorful J, his experiences of playing with almost everybody and his many jobs that define his personality as much as they do the city. He talks non-stop for a long time, his gold teeth flashing in the sun. Sweat helps you process his blues-drenched back-story.

Born James Monque Digby in Louisiana's Cajun country, he has French, Indian, and black blood—a Creole, however that widely misunderstood term is defined. His grandmother gave him a harmonica when he was four, "mostly to keep me from driving her crazy." Moving Uptown a year later, he learned the harmonica from his father, uncles, and grandmother. He started the J Monque'D band at age thirteen and had his first paying gig at Skateland, a roller skating rink on St. Claude Avenue. Within two years, he had already shared the stage with Muddy Waters and Lightning Hopkins. He later played with Professor Longhair

("I dated his youngest daughter"), John Lee Hooker, Earl King, Dr. John, "Frogman" Henry, Deacon John, Memphis Slim, Koko Taylor, and practically everyone else. He met the Beatles and saw Elvis, Jerry Lee Lewis, and Little Richard rehearse at the Dew Drop Inn. Since 1947, he seems to have met most of the Rock and Roll Hall of Fame.

His work experience is as extensive. After serving in Vietnam, J worked as a barker on Bourbon Street, as a carriage driver in the Quarter, and as a Lucky Dog street-vendor. If he wasn't in *The Confederacy of Dunces,* he should have been. He wrestled with "my own demons and beat them," battling substance abuse and serving a prison term for stalking his ex-wife. His musical career and talents have never waned—he has played every Jazz Fest, save two, and made nearly forty trips to Europe.

Now in an Uptown shotgun, he once lived on Tchoupitoulas Street near Tipitina's and for seven years on the same street as the Nevilles. He makes full use of his front porch, greeting his next-door neighbor and her newborn and chatting with his nephew, who is returning dishes to J and bringing him some food. He once told local columnist Angus Lind that his phone voice message went, "I eat the blues, I sleep the blues, I is the blues." Not a bad description of the reality of his wild and eclectic life.

DEACON JOHN MOORE

Listening to Deacon John spin tales of New Orleans music since 1952, it's impossible not to laugh. The Deacon is one of those people who regales his listeners with one story after another, the next one better than the last, laughing increasingly harder at himself. With a growing flock of lovebirds chirping in the kitchen ("someone gave me them at a gig, now I got more") and surrounded by instruments, the gentlemanly and gracious Moore is obviously comfortable in his Uptown home and studio.

None of this is surprising. This ageless Creole guitarist has been the soundtrack of New Orleans for decades: for blacks and whites, from the Ninth Ward to Uptown, and at weddings, proms, fraternity parties, and funerals. So great has been his local success that he has never really toured, saying, "I'm most proud that I have been able to earn a living as a musician right here in my hometown." And he gives back, serving as the first black president of the local Musicians Union.

Raised in a family of thirteen children near the Seventh Ward, Moore's classically-trained mother introduced him to music. "She thought I had the gift, mostly because I cried the loudest." Creole legend held that if you trimmed a child's fingernails under a fig tree, he or she would become a singer. Moore soon had short nails. He sang for his mother's church friends ("they gave me a dime, first paying gig"), which led to participating in the choir. But his concealed passion was R&B, to which Moore listened on his crystal radio, hiding under the covers with his headphones. Buying his first guitar for $20 at a Canal Street pawn shop, Moore played chords until his fingers bled; "I had to learn guitar, [it was a] much cooler way to meet girls than singing in church."

Moore started playing with the Ivories, where he was known as "Red." The bank thought its leader needed a more compelling nickname, and drummer Al Miller suggested "Deacon." Unaware that the name came from Roy Brown's R&B classic, "Good Rockin' Tonight," Red was horrified, exclaiming, "That ain't no nickname, that's a church name, we ain't ever going to get no gigs." The name stuck, however, and the band got plenty of gigs. And the Deacon prospered as a legendary sideman with musicians such as Allen Toussaint, Ernie K-Doe, Aaron Neville, and Fats Domino.

With his local chops firmly established, it was only fair that Deacon enjoyed some late-life national attention with the 2003 release of the critically acclaimed *Deacon John's Jump Blues*. But that did little to change Deacon, his self-deprecating sense of humor intact, his love for his city's musical heritage even more intense: "We different here—we dance different, we clap hands different, we can play anything, we are the most feared musicians in the world. And it's my home."

STANTON MOORE

Drummer Stanton Moore's studio is located just off of Tchoupitoulas Street within a block of the city's docks. These same docks have long provided work to New Orleans musicians. Pops Foster, George Lewis, Aaron Neville, and countless sidemen have labored long hours along the Mississippi to supplement their too-often inadequate musical earnings.

Moore fortunately does not have to work the docks, but the fact that the studio of one of the city's hardest working musicians is within sight of them seems appropriate. Landing an interview with the popular Galactic drummer took more than a year, mostly because of a schedule that had him touring constantly with four different bands, teaching classes, and producing records. Moore uses this warehouse studio to teach master classes, usually on Monday nights, when he serves his mother's legendary red beans and rice recipe. Road gear, thousands of CDs, countless drums, and even a motor boat are scattered around. The right side of the warehouse is a full recording studio and control room, used by Galactic to produce its last several records.

Moore grew up in Metairie. Going to Mardi Gras parades with his mother and "getting so excited when I heard the drums coming" convinced him by the time he was nine that he wanted to be a drummer.

He pursued this ambition in laser-like fashion. He went to Brother Martin High School because they had the best drum line in the city. There, he studied with revered band leader, Marty Hurley, who taught him discipline and how to "play rigid and tight."

Moore then went to Loyola for music and this time studied with Johnny Vidacovich, who "loosened me up musically" after Hurley's precise instruction. Moore appreciated drummers such as Russell Batiste and Zigaboo Modeliste to "help me get my right blend." By the time Moore helped to launch Galactic in the mid 1990s, he was well-grounded within the city's storied drumming tradition. A list of the bands with which Moore plays is daunting. Besides Galactic, he is involved with the Stanton Moore Trio, Dragon Smoke, Garage à Trois, Midnite Disturbers, and MG5.

Not surprisingly, the friendly and youthful Moore is as energetic off-stage as he is on-stage. He begins each day practicing the drums in his pajamas at his Algiers Point home. He skateboards to the bank and to the store and rides bikes in City Park with his wife. He confesses to an affinity for Legos. He tutors his seven-year-old daughter in the drums. On- and off-stage, Moore is keenly aware of the New Orleans music tradition, taking pride in his own role in preserving it.

ART NEVILLE

New Orleans is a city that is in part defined by the unique nature of its many iconic streets. There is Bourbon Street for revelry, Frenchmen for music, Canal for commerce, Elysian Fields for its streetcar, and St. Charles Avenue for its mansions. And then there is Valence Street, for decades given its identity as the home of keyboard player Art Neville and other members of his legendary family.

To spend time with a member of one of the first families of New Orleans music as a final session for this project seemed appropriate. Art Neville was born on Valence in 1937. Except for a few youthful years on Calliope, he has always lived on this very street, moving up and down to various houses, now living in a home that he bought from drummer Zigaboo Modeliste. He remembers when Valence was paved with oyster shells and he played with his brothers, "jumping in and out of the gutters." Even today, the Neville family owns five houses on the street.

Neville played his first piano on Valence in his aunt's house at 1012. He experimented some with the organ at the nearby Trinity Baptist Church. Influenced by Fats Domino, friends with James Booker, and an inspiration to Deacon John, Neville joined an R&B group, the Hawkettes, in 1953, contributing "Mardi Gras Mambo" to the city's musical library. After a stint in the navy, he came back to New Orleans and began playing with his brothers and other prominent musicians such as guitarist Leo Nocentelli, bassist George Porter, and drummer (and friend) Zigaboo Modeliste. Brothers Aaron and Cyril soon departed to pursue their own careers. Art, Nocentelli, Porter, and Modeliste morphed into the Meters, developing a unique funk-, R&B-, and jazz-inflected sound.

But there was the inevitability that the Nevilles would eventually reunite. Their uncle, George Landry, brought them together in 1976 to record "The Wild Tchoupitoulas" in homage to the city's Mardi Gras Indian tradition. With the eldest, Art, on the keyboard, Charles on sax, Cyril on percussion, and Aaron on vocals, the Neville Brothers soon began touring together, creating a distinctive sound that is part R&B, part soul, part funk, and all New Orleans. As a Meter and Neville Brother, two of New Orleans's most influential groups, Art Neville has a musical pedigree as fine as anyone's in the city.

Frequently sitting on his front porch to watch the passing scene, Neville still treasures life on Valence and on all of the streets of New Orleans. He has played with the Rolling Stones and entertained Queen Elizabeth. But his biggest thrill remains "winning a talent show outside Rosenwald Gym when I was a kid. My band backed out so I got up on the bed of an eighteen-wheeler and played an old upright piano. Sang 'Is it a Dream?' And damn if I didn't win." Neville smiles and reflects, "Life is enchanted. It's been good, man." For this musician, it's been enchanted and, evidently, not a dream.

CHARMAINE NEVILLE

Finding Charmaine Neville cooking in the kitchen of her Bywater home is hardly surprising. The popular jazz and R&B singer is every bit as devoted to good New Orleans food as she is to the city's music. On the day she was photographed, the youthful Charmaine (age not disclosed "but my birthday is March 31") was singlehandedly preparing a Neville family feast in celebration of her grandson's departure for college the next day. There would be thirty-one Nevilles at dinner, and Charmaine was determined to prepare every dish requested by her grandson. Seemingly unbothered by the August heat and lack of air-conditioning, the effervescent Neville insisted that the writer stir her lasagna sauce while she continued to prepare another ten dishes ("triple-chocolate bread pudding is good, but the deep-dish apple pie with three crusts is really what everybody comes for").

Like New Orleans, Charmaine understands the artful impact of a good mix of food and music, often giving her cookies to the audience before her regular Monday-night gig at Snug Harbor. In 2010, she opened Charmaine's Place, her own club and restaurant where she was "the entertainment, the waitress, the cashier, the bouncer, the dishwasher, and the cook."

Daughter of Charles Neville, saxophonist for the Neville Brothers, Neville moved from New Orleans to Austin, where she began performing when she was twelve. She returned to her hometown when she was sixteen, only then starting to fully appreciate the extent of her family's musical heritage and the role of her father, uncles, and cousins in fashioning the city's unique sounds. She played with her father and backed up the Neville Brothers, then did a stint with the Survivors, whose members included Harry Connick Jr. and Bobby McFerrin. She eventually created the Charmaine Neville Band with saxophonist Reggie Miller and pianist Amasa Miller, developing her own international identity as one of the city's most caring and charismatic performers.

Neville was one of the most outspoken and passionate voices of protest after Hurricane Katrina. Second lines, festivals, benefits—the ubiquitous Charmaine seldom misses an opportunity to speak up for the city's musicians and the restoration of a tradition that she claims "they may have tried to kill, but we are just coming back stronger. That's New Orleans."

CYRIL NEVILLE

Vocalist and percussionist Cyril Neville, one of the famed Neville Brothers, wishes it would rain. Barefoot and relaxed, he is tending to his garden at the home he shares with his wife and family in Slidell, across Lake Pontchartrain from New Orleans. An unusual dry spell has Neville continually casting his eyes at gathering storm-clouds, hopeful they will provide some relief for his crop of cucumbers, beans, and tomatoes.

Known for his passionate political and philosophical opinions, Neville at first might seem out of place in a pastoral setting. But image does not always reflect reality. Gentle and warm, he does his gardening barefoot because "it allows me to reconnect with the earth." He is surrounded by family on the three-acre property, including his wife, Gaynielle (also a musician), and daughter, Liryca ("that's Cyril spelled backwards with an 'a' on the end"). He proudly sports his tattoos, noting that the first one he ever got was with musician and lifelong friend, George Porter Jr.

Born in 1948, the youngest of four brothers, Neville grew up on Valence Street in Uptown New Orleans. As the city's R&B, funk, and rock scene exploded, he was engulfed by music, explaining, "my brothers always playing, Deacon John, Allen Toussaint, seemed like pretty much everybody was a musician." At age nineteen, he began to make money playing music, singing with his brothers Art and Aaron in clubs around town. He eventually became a member of Art's band, the Meters, and toured with the Rolling Stones in 1974.

The four Neville brothers collaborated on the 1976 release, *Wild Tchoupitoulas*, a call-and-response album in the style of the city's Mardi Gras Indians, produced by the ubiquitous Allen Toussaint. This effort encouraged the brothers to perform together, and the Neville Brothers eventually became one of the city's most recognized and revered acts. The city's recovery from Katrina never really felt right until 2008, when the Nevilles returned to their traditional spot as the closing act for Jazz Fest. Experimenting with blues, reggae, and rock, Cyril has also maintained a successful solo career. Through the years, he has played with a number of bands, including his self-titled Cyril Neville & Tribe 13, the Voice of the Wetlands All-Stars, and Royal Southern Brotherhood. Fiercely devoted to the financial interests of his fellow musicians, Neville has a strong social conscience.

So closely identified with New Orleans, a city which both delights and frustrates him, Neville laughs that even with all the music around him at home, "First time I ever saw Dr. John play, I was walking by Carnegie Hall with my brothers and saw he was playing that night. We hung around for sound-check, finally got to talk to him, and saw his show." Out of all the lousy juke-joints in the world, Cyril saw Dr. John for the first time at Carnegie Hall. As Cyril and his brothers realize, the music of their hometown travels far and it travels well.

FREDY OMAR

The reigning king of the city's vibrant Latin music scene, singer Fredy Omar, lives in the Ninth Ward's Musicians' Village. With its mixture of New Orleans musicians, young and old, native and newcomer, it is a fitting home for the Honduran native who so successfully blends his Latin sound with the underlying rhythms of his adopted hometown.

At home, Omar is reserved, a long way from his charismatic stage performances that inevitably get his audiences on their feet dancing. He loves the city's artistic diversity and creative opportunities: "This place is like a musical theme park." He explains, "If a musician can't make it here, he won't be able to make it anywhere." Like so many of his fellow musicians, he especially values the chances to appear on stage with bands playing all different styles of music.

Omar came to New Orleans in 1992 at age twenty-two, unable to speak a word of English. In Honduras, he began singing early, taking inspiration from his grandfather's huge collection of salsa and meringue music. He was classically trained at the National School of Music and started touring in Honduras and El Salvador, singing romantic ballads and bolero. But musical opportunities in Central America were limited, so when the New Orleans promoters of a Honduran music festival in the Quarter offered him a spot on the bill, he traveled north.

The festival never took place, but Omar never left. He began playing with some of the area's Latin bands. In 1997, he started his own band, Fredy Omar con su Banda. Most of the band members were long time veterans of the Latin jazz scene. Their experience, combined with Omar's own dynamic creativity, resulted in a sound that combined traditional Latin dance rhythms with New Orleans funk and jazz. Omar released several albums, opened for Jimmy Buffet, and has been a "must see" fixture of Jazz Fest since 1998. "The Latin King of Frenchmen Street," Omar regularly packs clubs such as the Blue Nile and the old Café Brasil.

New Orleans has been called the northernmost city of Latin America. It can trace much of its musical heritage to Africa and Cuba, genres that Omar freely admits inspire him. It is not surprising that Omar would feel at home here. And it is important for the city's continually evolving musical scene to have him. New Orleans music has always relied upon cultural fusion, especially from the south. Omar is doing his part to keep that tradition alive.

ANDERS OSBORNE

A relaxed Anders Osborne is cooking breakfast in his home near City Park and offering his visitors some eggs, obviously enjoying his down-time in the house from 1889 that he shares with his wife and two children. The blues and rock guitarist and vocalist is only the third owner of the house and is in the process of a long and meticulous renovation to open up the floor plan and enhance the natural light. He understands that in New Orleans, you never really own an old home, explaining, "At most, I'm just the custodian of something that belongs to the whole city."

The attention that Osborne devotes to the restoration of his home reflects the approach he gives to preserving his personal life. Osborne freely admits that he has long battled substance-abuse problems. Now clean and an active runner, Osborne talks openly of his recovery program, the strength of his family, and the importance of his daily routine in keeping himself straight.

Another musician from somewhere else who really was always meant to be in New Orleans, the blues-loving Osborne is a Swede who grew up around music (presumably not ABBA). He found Sweden too confining, and so by sixteen, he began a hitchhiking odyssey through Europe, the Middle East, and Asia. While in Dubrovnik, he met a fellow traveler who was from New Orleans. After spending time together in Greece and Egypt, the two separated with a vow to reunite in a year in New Orleans. The first time Osborne saw the city, in 1985, approaching from across Lake Pontchartrain, he knew immediately, "This place is special, this is some real s---, and I had been all over the world."

Osborne plunged into the city and its music, writing his deeply personal, blues-tinged melodies, now playing a slide guitar. He opened for Earl King at Tipitina's ("the Holy Grail of New Orleans"), played with George Porter, and toured with the Subdudes. Renowned for intensely energetic concerts, he collaborated with a variety of musicians, ranging from Tim McGraw, for whom he wrote a number-one hit, to Keb' Mo', whose 1999 Grammy Award-winning album included two songs written by Osborne. A member of the Voice of the Wetlands All-Stars along with Tab Benoit, Dr. John, and others, Osborne is as dedicated to the preservation of the wetlands as he is to the city's musical traditions.

Osborne is very open and quick to share his feelings and convictions. He freely admits that Katrina had a huge impact on his personal life and his music. He lost friends and fought depression and his addictions. But he survived. He concludes, "The storm was just so damn big, almost biblical. To me, there really is no pre-Katrina, only post. It created in me an urgency to live a good life, to recommit to my music, to make it simpler. Though the trauma is still alive for everyone, I wouldn't be where I am today, as a person or musician, if it hadn't been for that awful storm."

NICHOLAS PAYTON

Trumpeter Nicholas Payton is a few minutes late for our meeting in Jackson Square, which is more than understandable given his extraordinarily busy schedule. Recently returned from a European tour that included stops in Zurich, Istanbul, and Belgium, Payton is also a Distinguished Artist and Lecturer for 2011-2012 at Tulane University and continues to release highly acclaimed recordings that push the creative envelope.

But Payton has chosen Jackson Square for his photograph in tribute to his musical roots. As a youngster not tied to any schedule, he used to busk for tips in front of the Square's St. Louis Cathedral. And one of his first gigs was right up the street at the Famous Door on Bourbon Street. He explains, "Right down here in the Quarter is a big part of where I grew up."

Payton, born in 1973, is the son of bassist and sousaphonist Walter Payton, who introduced him to the horn at age four. By the time Nicholas was nine, he was playing with his father, Greg Stafford, and Michael White in the Young Tuxedo Brass Band. He went to NOCCA and eventually to the University of New Orleans, where, like so many others of the city's musicians, he studied with Ellis Marsalis.

By the mid-1990s, Payton's recording career began to take off. In 1997, he won a Grammy Award. He has played with Wynton Marsalis, Clark Terry, Roy Haynes, and recently with Dr. John at highly praised concerts held in New York's Brooklyn Academy of Music. Along with the trumpet, he has mastered the piano, often playing the horn with his right hand and the keys with his left. In his most recent release, the provocatively-titled *Bitches,* Payton played all of the instruments, wrote all of the lyrics, and composed all of the music.

Reserved and intensely intellectual, Payton rejects "jazz" as a marketing label that fails to capture the many dimensions of the black musical experience. He prefers to call his music "BAM," which stands for Black American Music and represents an amalgam of jazz, blues, soul, and hip-hop. Payton is also a prolific and outspoken blogger, passionate about issues of race, politics, and music. While not everyone agrees with him, his spirited argument in favor of Louis Armstrong (and not Michael Jackson) as the real King of Pop is a strong defense of the musical heritage of his hometown. And unlike some musicians, Payton embraces political controversy, making his choice of Jackson Square, the seat of Louisiana's first government, perhaps even more appropriate.

MARGIE PEREZ

*H*anging in the kitchen of multi-talented fusion singer Margie Perez's Musicians' Village home is a photograph of Perez shaking Barack Obama's hand. Displayed prominently on her coffee table is a two-by-four-inch piece of wood autographed by Obama. A native of the Washington, DC, area, Perez only began hanging out with aspiring presidential candidates after she moved to New Orleans. These are the kind of opportunities her adopted hometown has provided.

Perez met the president-to-be in 2008 when he toured Habitat for Humanity's Musicians' Village, where Perez had qualified for a house. She was putting in her sweat equity when she encountered a campaigning Obama. He signed her photograph and a newspaper photographer snapped their picture. Several months later, when the Democratic convention was looking for a speaker to represent New Orleans, someone remembered the vivacious and attractive Perez and asked her to speak at the Denver confabulation.

Perez is the child of Cuban immigrants who came to the DC area in 1959. She grew up listening to Cuban music, a good foundation for someone who one day would end up in New Orleans. Working as a travel agent and singing recreationally, she first fell in love with the city when she came to Jazz Fest in 1994. Ten straight trips to Jazz Fest followed until she decided, after a divorce, that she needed a change and relocated to New Orleans nine months before Katrina. Almost immediately, she began sitting in with bands on Frenchmen Street. She says, "I just found the musicians here so approachable. They just welcomed me." Blues singer Marva Wright mentored her and Allen Toussaint invited her to be a backup singer for his 2006 Jazz Fest performance.

The versatile Perez soon earned a reputation for enthusiastic experimentation, willing to try any style and work with any group. After she returned to the city post-storm, she quit her day job, determined to make a living as a musician. She started her own band, joined the African jazz-fusion group Ensemble Fatien, and sang with the Afro-Cuban ensemble Moyuba. She also fronts for the Ibervillians, a psychedelic band. After she released a CD with Threadhead Records, her latest project is the Honeypots, where she combines her song-writing skills and lyrical voice with the talents of guitarist Lynn Drury and cellist Monica McIntyre.

Engaged politically and a passionate defender of New Orleans, Perez also loves her Musicians' Village home. She likes her front porch and the chance to chat with her neighbors and to learn from the other musicians. And she speaks with wonder how her life has turned out: "For me to be such a fan of Jazz Fest and then end up playing there—that kind of thing just isn't supposed to happen."

ALBINAS PRIZGINTAS

The informal nature of Albinas Prizgintas's Jackson Avenue apartment seems worlds apart from the stately Trinity Episcopal Church where he has been the organist and musical director since 1988. But both reflect who he is—after all, very few can claim to have met Einstein as a child, graduated from Juilliard, won a Fulbright Scholarship, played with Memphis Slim, and been a close friend of Ernie K-Doe, the fabled Emperor of the Universe.

Trinity provides the apartment for Prizgintas and his French wife, Manon. Visitors are welcome so long as they remove their shoes. Scattered around the den are Prizgintas's compositional notes as he sits on the floor and practices on a keyboard, using earphones to avoid disturbing the neighbors and to block out the sounds of the children playing at nearby Trinity School.

Born in Germany to Lithuanian parents, Prizgintas immigrated to the United States as a young child. His father took him to meet Einstein, living in nearby Princeton. His mother was the organist in a Catholic church and encouraged Prizgintas to play piano and then organ. After Juilliard, he won a Fulbright to study French classical organ techniques in Europe. After returning to the States, he developed a passion for the blues, playing in New York clubs. He eventually returned to Paris, where he met Memphis Slim in a deserted bistro. A fast friendship ensued and they played together in Paris and New York. His classical organist career prospered with a position at a church in Brooklyn and concerts in St. Patrick's Cathedral on Fifth Avenue.

With Prizgintas's eclectic interests and talents, New Orleans eventually beckoned to him. After taking the Trinity job, he brought local music right into the old-line sanctuary with his Trinity Artist series, featuring gospel choirs and R&B greats such as Earl King and Harold Battiste. He shared his considerable talents with the community—seven years as the house pianist at Henry Lee's Genghis Khan restaurant and then four years with the Yellowdog Blues Band at Joe's House of Blues in Central City. He directed the Kingsley House of Blues Festival, worked with Marva Wright and Eddie Bo, and became so close to Ernie K-Doe and his wife, Antoinette, that he made them godparents of his son.

There are many sides to Prizgintas. Reserved and intellectual, he is the more-than-capable custodian of the rich classical tradition at Trinity Episcopal. But he is also passionate and unexpectedly fiery, claiming, "The first time I ever came to New Orleans, I got in a fight on Bourbon Street." Very little about this city and its diverse set of musicians surprises.

JOHN RANKIN

Jazz guitarist John Rankin is a comfortable man—friendly, informal, and eager to share his many experiences with New Orleans musicians. His 1920s Mid-City home on an oak-lined street near Bayou St. John reflects his personality. Family and pets wander through the living room during the interview. Two caged birds greet visitors from a well-used front porch. The interview moves from room to room—from kitchen to living room to porch to Rankin's studio, where he stores his twenty-two guitars. The six-foot-six Rankin is a gracious host, regaling his visitors with anecdotes about musical legends such as Danny Barker and Snooks Eaglin.

Rankin loves to teach guitar, which he does at three local universities, and give plenty of private lessons. His home has the feel of a place where music is cherished and its traditions honored. Rankin comes by this honestly: his father was a music-loving professor at Tulane University, and his mother was a jazz archivist who also moonlighted as a WWOZ DJ, the beloved Big Mama, which was a gig that always gave her son lots of "street cred."

Not surprisingly, Big Mama had a lot to do with Rankin's musical career. She took him as a teenager to see Louis Armstrong, a performance that "literally made my hair stand on end." Listening to her records, he taught himself to play the guitar and juggled various Bourbon Street gigs as a teenager. By the mid-1970s, he had drifted to New England, where he attended the Berklee School of Music and worked in construction. Big Mama intervened again, this time sending him a plane ticket to come to the 1976 Jazz Fest.

That Jazz Fest proved to be one of Rankin's "periodic musical epiphanies." The music of local musicians such as Henry Butler, Johnny Vidacovich, and Leo Nocentelli mesmerized him. He realized he needed to get back home; "to find my identity, I needed to get back to a city with an identity." He returned within two years and has since had a successful career as a guitarist, using a unique left-handed style to play classical, jazz, blues, folk, and New Age.

The city's musical talent continues to fascinate Rankin. "People [such as] Tom McDermott and Steve Masakowski and the music they play simply amaze me," he says. Rankin's return home ensured that he would become a valuable part of that same tradition.

KATEY RED

The pioneering queen of New Orleans sissy bounce, Katey Red, is waiting on the porch of her shotgun home not far from Tulane Avenue. The landmark Falstaff brewery sign is visible around the corner. It is one of those February days when New Orleans can be surprisingly cold. Katey climbs into the front seat of her SUV, turns the heat all the way up, lights up, and conducts her interview with the driver's-side window only partially open.

Katey is striking: tall and attractive. New Orleans bounce music, distinctive and regional, features raw and repetitive beats with equally repetitive lyrics that are practically always hypersexual. She is insistent that "sissy bounce is the wrong name. It is just bounce music, [with] sissies doing it." The music is call-and-response based and heavily influenced by Mardi Gras Indian chants. It is hyper-kinetic, a "music that makes you bounce it: girls like to shake it, guys like to watch it" (visuals readily available on YouTube).

Born Kenyon Carter in 1981, Katey was raised in the Melpomene housing projects. Fond of dolls and nail polishing and a majorette in her high school marching band, Katey began taking female hormones not long after the release of her first album in 2000. DJ Jubilee discovered her in 1998 when she took the stage at an underground club near the projects where she grew up, "not sure once I got up there if they would beat me up or not." She signed with the prestigious Take Fo' Records label and released a couple of albums. Her song "Melpomene Block Party" was a breakout hit.

Before long, Katey was crossing over from the city's drag clubs occasionally to go mainstream, performing at Jazz Fest, Voodoo Fest, and South by Southwest. She was the first sissy bounce breakout star and is the only one who consistently performs dressed·as a woman. Her friend, Big Freedia, now a star in his own right, was once one of Katey's backup singers. Still very much part of the New Orleans street scene, Katey has also worked with bands such as Galactic and singers such as Irma Thomas.

New Orleans is a city that is as welcome to gays and cross-dressers as it is to its musical mainstream. With Mardi Gras, masking, and the city's libertine atmosphere, gender identity is sometimes a mixed bag. Katey says, "Even two year olds here learn how to shake it in their diapers." It is the right city for sissy bounce, one form of rap to make inroads into a notoriously homophobic hip-hop community. But it is still very much a medium of the streets, where hostilities towards homosexuals can be rampant. Katey also lives in a neighborhood where strangers stand out. As we talk, a wary Katey notes that we may be attracting some attention of the wrong kind and that it is probably time to leave. Not ones to argue, we pack up, aware that in certain neighborhoods, Katey may be performing even when she is not on stage.

COCO ROBICHEAUX

*P*rominently displayed on the mantle of the modest Faubourg Marigny home in which Coco Robicheaux lived was a framed letter from the actual owner of the house, which gave Coco the right to live there indefinitely. The gracious note is typical of the kind of loyalty that the colorful and beloved Robicheaux inspired.

Part Cajun, part Choctaw, Robicheaux greeted visitors with a voodoo handshake, dressed in a black leather jacket and hat with blue leather pants. Scattered around the house were voodoo shrines, eagle feathers, Native American and folk art, instruments, and stacks of old CDs. There was not a lot of furniture, but Robicheaux really didn't seem to mind. Deeply mystical, he was more interested in sharing the contents of his lucky gris-gris pouch—an alligator tooth, an acorn, a small animal skull, and a dead cockroach.

Born in 1947 as Curtis Arceneaux and raised in the bayou's Ascension Parish, Robicheaux denied the popular legend that he took his name from a Dr. John song, declaring, "Ain't true, I got it from a Cajun story about a little boy, Coco Robicheaux, who ignored his parents and made the mistake of looking right at a loup garou [werewolf]." First playing the trombone, he switched to the guitar after the Beatles revolutionized music, saying that "After them, if you wanted to get laid, you had to play the guitar." By age fifteen, he was in New Orleans gigging in the Quarter. In the 1960s, the free-spirited Robicheaux made his way to San Francisco, where he met Janis Joplin at a free health clinic where he worked. He returned to New Orleans not long afterwards to play with Dr. John and Willy DeVille and eventually carved out an itinerant and successful hoodoo blues career with his distinctive growl of a voice and a guitar style to match.

Robicheaux unabashedly shared his voodoo beliefs, especially within the city's second line culture and its unorthodox celebrations of death. Outside of his music, he also acted, with a memorable role as himself in HBO's *Treme*. He claimed that a producer recently approached him for a role as a television bad guy: "They needed someone without teeth; bad guys never have all their teeth, that's me." But he always appreciated where he lived, saying, "Every damn musician in this city is good, it's a warranty. You come from New Orleans, you can play."

Coco Robicheaux died suddenly on November 25, 2011, collapsing in front of his favorite Frenchmen Street haunt, the Apple Barrel. According to a close friend, his last words were, "I'm home."

WANDA ROUZAN

Although known for its snowballs, New Orleans has more than one refreshing, cold treat to combat its steamy and sultry summers. In the Seventh Ward, where R&B singer Wanda Rouzan grew up, they had the hucklebuck, frozen fruit cups consumed so voraciously by the young Creole girl that she ended up with "Hucklebuck" as her nickname. Making her visitors at home in her Tonti Street house, Rouzan shares her last hucklebuck with the photographer.

Rouzan's home is in the heart of the city's historic Creole area. Except for her education, she has lived her entire life in the Tonti and Annette Street neighborhood. Rebuilding her house after eight feet of Katrina flooding from the hurricane, Rouzan is gracious and full of a fierce spirit and pride. From the way she has decorated her house, much of that pride is manifested in her dedication to the New Orleans Saints.

Rouzan had a 1950 and 1960s childhood full of music "in the streets, on our porches, in our churches." She has an encyclopedic memory of those years—of the Bouttés, Wardell Quezergue, Danny White, Irma Thomas ("my idol"), the Louisiana Purchase, the Dixie Cups, and her dad's close friend, Lionel Ferbos. Performing ever since she was four, Rouzan sang with her sisters, Barbara and Laura, winning talent shows all over the city. The trio backed up Danny White on his hit "Kiss Tomorrow Goodbye."

After graduating from Xavier University and earning a masters in speech pathology from Pennsylvania State University, Rouzan returned to New Orleans and did some musical theater. David Lastie convinced her to resume her singing career, which has led to international acclaim as the R&B "Sweetheart of New Orleans." After Lastie's death, his family passed on the name of his band, "A Taste of New Orleans," to Rouzan, who uses it to this day. Still teaching theater at a charter school in the city, she was one of the first female grand marshals of a jazz funeral. She is deeply respectful of that tradition, saying, "I won't help cut anyone loose and take them home unless I knew them and loved them."

Rouzan considers music "a type of therapy that soothes our soul, especially since the storm." She began her interview by playing the signature love song that she wrote about the city, "Come on Down to My New Orleans." With a warm laugh, she finishes it by telling the interviewer that she has to go and make more hucklebucks. She may have lost the nickname, but she has kept her appetite.

KERMIT RUFFINS

Standing outside of Sidney's Saloon, the bar and club he operates on St. Bernard Avenue in the city's Seventh Ward, Kermit Ruffins is a popular neighborhood figure, the object of plenty of waves, honking horns and "hello, good morning" greetings. People are reacting to more than the musical talents of Ruffins, the latest embodiment of New Orleans's street-brass tradition. As usual, Ruffins is cooking right on the street, his crew preparing the grills for his famous barbecue and stirring pots full of crawfish, shrimp, sausage, and potatoes. Unfazed by all the activity, the famously relaxed Ruffins put on a tie, re-did his do-rag, added his trademark fedora, and was almost ready for his photograph. But he went to grab his trumpet, a big part of "being Kermit Ruffins" even when he is not on stage.

Identifying with the streets and clubs of the city, Ruffins does not confine his musical and culinary skills to Sidney's. He plays 250 gigs per year, mostly in New Orleans, with a legendary Thursday-night gig at Vaughan's in the Bywater, which features his music, his barbecue, his favorite beverage (Bud Light), and occasionally other recreational pleasures as well. Possessed with the same kind of musical self-confidence as now-deceased Emperor of the Universe, Ernie K-Doe, Ruffins recently signed a lease to re-open K-Doe's Mother-in-Law Lounge on Claiborne Avenue.

A native of the Ninth Ward and now living in the Bywater, Ruffins was born in 1964 (on December 19, the same day as Professor Longhair). Like many others, he honed his trumpet-playing skills marching in his high school band and then taking his skills to the French Quarter to busk for tips. In 1983, he co-founded the Rebirth Brass Band, eventually recording seven albums with them in a recognizable and influential brass-jazz-funk style until his amicable departure in 1992. Since then, he has fronted his own funk-jazz quintet, the Barbecue Swingers.

Ruffins is quick to honor his musical predecessors: "My hero is Louis Armstrong, no question, but Tuba Fats, Benny Jones, Uncle Lionel, Danny Barker, all those guys are right up there." And he recognizes his ensuing responsibility to the city's musical heritage, saying, "There ain't nothing like this scene, it's so big. And last three years I understood my responsibility to keep it going, ain't going to let it die."

PAUL SANCHEZ

ayarre Place is a small park in New Orleans at the intersection of Esplanade Avenue and Bayou Road. It honors nineteenth-century New Orleans historian Charles Gayarre, best known for his comprehensive histories of Louisiana. In the center of the park is a statute of Ceres, the ancient goddess of fertility, first on display in 1884 at the Cotton Exposition in Audubon Park. Guitarist and prolific songwriter Paul Sanchez chose to be photographed in Gayarre Place, a spot that provides him with creative inspiration—to good effect, as Sanchez has recently carved out a seemingly ubiquitous role in the post-Katrina musical community.

Sanchez adapted Dan Baum's *Nine Lives,* a book about the impact of Hurricanes Betsy and Katrina on nine New Orleanians, to the musical stage. He leads the self-titled "whoever shows up" New Orleans ensemble, Paul Sanchez and the Rolling Road Show. He mentors younger musicians such as Shamarr Allen and Glen David Andrews, all while writing songs as well as anyone in the city, playing the clubs, and recording with friends such as John Boutté. That Sanchez would want to be photographed in a park on Esplanade in the midst of mid-day traffic shows why he is as open and approachable as any musician in town.

The laconic and casual Sanchez was born in 1961 in the Irish Channel as one of eleven children. Music on the radio permeated their lives. He says, "It was like a gift to the poor." Sanchez's longshoreman father died when Sanchez was only five, and he took deeper refuge in music, explaining that "It felt better to sing than to cry." Playing the guitar, Sanchez spent time as a musician in New York City in the 1980s before returning to New Orleans to launch a successful rock career with the Backbeats and then Cowboy Mouth for sixteen years.

When Katrina hit, Sanchez was on the road with Cowboy Mouth. He says, "A friend told me after the storm I could be a better man or a worse man, but I could never be the same man." Sanchez left Cowboy Mouth and began to re-forge his connections to the city's music. He explains that in order "To find myself, I had to return to my roots." For his journey, Sanchez relied upon other New Orleans musicians. Spencer Bohren convinced him to stick with music. David Torkanowsky persuaded him to learn more about jazz. John Rankin gave him guitar lessons. And John Boutté reintroduced him to the streets of Treme, where he now lives with his wife, Shelly.

TOM SANCTON

The French Quarter may seem an unusual locale to encounter a Harvard-educated Rhodes Scholar with a PhD from Oxford. But jazz clarinetist and writer Tom Sancton has an unusual background, even by New Orleans standards. He is obviously comfortable in the Quarter, a place that through the years has provided him with every bit as much education as the Ivy League.

Dressed in a dark suit and tie, the traditional attire of a jazz man, Sancton is on his way to a gig at the Palm Court Café, not far from Preservation Hall, where he first began learning the clarinet as a thirteen-year-old in 1962. His father had taken him there to introduce him to the older legends of traditional jazz that played the Hall in its early days. When Sancton heard George Lewis play "Burgundy Street Blues," he felt that "it was an epiphany, the hair on the back of my neck stood up." Epiphany notwithstanding, his parents then took the young Tom to Brocato's for an Italian ice cream.

The visit to Preservation Hall launched what Sancton has called "a lifelong musical apprenticeship learning from the masters." Playing in second lines and street funerals, sitting in at Preservation Hall (often the only white face in the band), Sancton was a willing pupil of Lewis and influenced by Albert Burbank and Louis Cottrell, each a New Orleans clarinet legend. Sancton went to Harvard and then Oxford, playing on the side with various bands such as the Black Eagles while he continued his studies.

He ended up in France researching his thesis and eventually met his wife, Sylvaine, appropriately enough at a New Orleans second line in Paris.

With characteristic intensity, Sancton decided in 1974 that he could not balance the demands of his research and career with occasional music, so he quit playing completely for twelve years while he went to work as a writer for *Time* magazine. A reunion in 1986 with his old band, the Black Eagles, rekindled the musical spark, and he continued to play off and on during the next twenty years, mostly in France, where he was the Paris bureau chief for *Time* until 2001. He then wrote *A Song for My Fathers: a New Orleans Story in Black and White,* chronicling his early days at Preservation Hall.

Living just outside Paris with his wife, seemingly an ex-pat for life, Sancton ultimately could not resist the lure of his hometown and the Quarter. After Hurricane Katrina hit and the need to help his aging parents grew, Sancton decided to return, a decision facilitated by a teaching opportunity as the Andrew Mellon Professor in the Humanities at Tulane University. He now plays over one hundred gigs per year, mostly in the Quarter. "Music lured me back," he says. "Katrina was pivotal; I wanted to help make sure that we didn't lose our music, our culture, our soul. This city is about coming together to have fun, to sing about our collective story. I wanted to be part of that again."

CHRISTIAN SCOTT

*I*sidore Newman High School in the summer is a busy place, with camps for jocks, theater geeks, and (not surprisingly in New Orleans) jazz musicians. Among the jazz instructors is trumpeter Christian Scott, who took time out from his teaching to be photographed in the school's courtyard.

The undeniably hip Scott, a self-described "fashionista," is youthful enough to be mistaken for a student. His musical interests reflect a strong intellect and deep curiosity. A graduate of the New Orleans Center for Creative Arts and the Berklee College of Music, Scott is a prodigy—completing a combined nine years of study at both schools in only five. He talks knowledgeably about the influence of Senegalese rhythms on the Mardi Gras Indians, Louis Armstrong, and Kid Ory; trends in progressive jazz; and the New Orleans bounce scene.

Scott is a Harrison, another one of the first families of New Orleans music. His grandfather was Big Chief Donald Harrison Sr. and his uncle and hero is Donald Harrison Jr. A spy boy in his grandfather's Mardi Gras Indian tribe, Scott grew up in the Ninth Ward, in the same house where his Uncle Donald

was raised. He received a trumpet at age twelve, an unusual gift in a family of reed players, but Scott knew that Uncle Donald needed a trumpet player in his band. Under the intense and demanding tutelage of his uncle, Scott worked his way into the band by the time he was fifteen.

Scott now lives in New York City, where he has been heralded as the architect of a new kind of jazz. His custom-made trumpet (named Katrina) has an upturned bell and is modeled after an idea Scott got from Dizzy Gillespie. A hard and demanding worker, he perfected his "whisper technique" after two years of virtual seclusion. "I use the air in my diaphragm to create a fuzzy and hazy sound. It makes you lean in to hear the horn whisper, no need to shout."

Scott returns to New Orleans five or six times a year, "to get grounded." He explains, "New York is about the individual; music in this city is about community. I need that." His teaching is part of that community. Creative, confident, and definitely smooth, Scott showed all of that during the 2011 Jazz Fest when he called his girlfriend onstage and proposed to her in front of a raucous audience. She said yes.

AMANDA SHAW

After only two hours of sleep the night before and a show earlier that evening, fiddler and singer Amanda Shaw claims to be "not totally together" when she arrives for her interview and photo shoot. But there was no way to tell. Speaking in the sing-song style of many young women (albeit with a pronounced Southern inflection), even a tired Amanda is full of enthusiasm and good cheer, reflecting someone with extraordinary talent who appreciates everything that she has experienced throughout her already extensive career.

Part of Shaw's delight is no doubt attributed to the spot she has selected for her photograph, the Magazine Street studio and shop of the young designer who helps assemble her outfits for shows. Even a tired Shaw is still capable of a clothes high, laughing infectiously about some wardrobe malfunctions she has had while performing (although for the innocent Shaw, none rivaled Janet Jackson's Super Bowl mishap).

Born in Boston in 1990, she moved to Covington on the North Shore when she was very young, and at four, Shaw was captivated by the violin while watching an orchestra on TV. She proved to be a prodigy, becoming, at age eight, the youngest soloist ever to play with the Baton Rouge Symphony Orchestra. Appearances on the *Rosie O'Donnell Show* in 1999 and 2001 followed. Her parents exposed her to all kinds of music: funk, soul, Cajun, zydeco, and blues. She ditched her classical training when she was nine and began fiddling with jazz, blues, and Cajun bands. Mitchell Reed, now of Beausoleil, was a mentor. At age ten, Shaw fronted her own band, later to be named the Cute Guys.

Shaw continues to expand her repertoire, now an eclectic and electric combination of Cajun, country, rock, blues, and folk. Her inspirations are diverse, ranging from Billie Holiday to Etta James to Bonnie Raitt to the late Amy Winehouse. Shaw has released several albums for various labels, including Rounder. A popular performer at venues such as Rock 'N' Bowl, Shaw has been attracting record crowds at Jazz Fest since she was ten.

Shaw tours all over the world but claims to "be a New Orleans girl all the way." She continues, "There is just no place like this city. New Orleans is the reason I love my job so much." And when given the chance, Shaw proved her point. As a teenager, she performed in two Disney television movies and was then offered the role of Hannah Montana (eventually taken by Miley Cyrus). Shaw says that doing the movies made her realize how much she loved music. So instead of Disney, she signed with Rounder. She has no regrets; after all, she has New Orleans.

JAMES SINGLETON

New Orleans in July suffocates, made barely livable by snow balls and air-conditioning. So when it came time to meet with jazz bassist James Singleton in his home on Bayou St. John, he naturally had his air-conditioning off and his windows open. But no one noticed the heat—Singleton is so engaging and animated that artificial air somehow would only have diminished his authenticity.

Singleton's reputation as one of the city's most intellectual and experimental musicians is reflected in his informal home, with thousands of CDs and books on every imaginable topic scattered about. He greets his visitors on a front porch full of bicycles. As we talk, his wife, Marcela, and their three-year-old daughter, Ruby, play on the floor while Tula the Dog wanders in and out.

Singleton came to New Orleans in 1977, taking the long route through Illinois, Massachusetts, and Texas. Born in Springfield, Illinois, in 1956, Singleton went to Boston's Berklee School of Music, where he met New Orleans natives David Torkanowsky and Steve Masakowski. That early connection, however, did not bring him to the city. He left Boston and ended up in college in Texas. He had the chance to back up Gatemouth Brown, saying, "At first I thought the music stunk, but after two songs, I was hooked." He moved to New Orleans; played with Fess, James Booker, and Ellis Marsalis; and before long, cemented a reputation as one of the city's most unconventional and experimental musicians.

Singleton in 1978 reunited with Masakowski and Torkanowsky and, along with Johnny Vidacovich, joined Tony Dagradi's Astral Project. The Project is distinguished for its improvisation and its distinctive blend of jazz, funk, and rock. Insatiably curious and eager for new challenges, Singleton pushes himself in new directions, playing with all sorts of groups such as Illuminati, 3 Now 4, the Robert Wagner Trio, and his self-titled James Singleton String Quartet.

After Katrina, Singleton tried Los Angeles but missed the "transcendent, almost spiritual quality" of his adopted hometown. He moved back into his Bayou St. John home, convinced that "it has been the music that has preserved and resurrected the town since the storm." And the youthful looking father keeps pushing himself, even learning to play the trumpet again after an absence of many years.

BARRY SMITH

*I*t's the week after Jazz Fest, and Barry Smith, owner of the Louisiana Music Factory in the French Quarter, finally can relax. For Smith and LMF, an independent record store specializing in New Orleans music, Jazz Fest is like "the Christmas season." Fans flock to the Factory with its knee-deep collection of New Orleans jazz, R&B, blues, Cajun, and zydeco records. Artists such as Robert Plant, in town to play at Jazz Fest, make surprise visits. The many in-store shows with musicians such as Trombone Shorty, Galactic, and Little Freddy King fill the aisles and the surrounding streets.

All of this keeps the genteel Smith from attending Jazz Fest to see the musicians that he so diligently features and promotes. Although he has never played an instrument ("I think I screwed around with a guitar once, but who hasn't?"), he is an essential part of the city's musical community. Fans of New Orleans music can be intensely loyal and idiosyncratic. Having a store in the heart of the Quarter that specializes in local music and has "physical product" enhances the New Orleans experience for such fans. And with a busy schedule of in-store shows going back to the 1990s, Smith has built abiding relationships with many of the city's musicians, affording them important promotional opportunities.

It wasn't always this way for the youthful-looking Smith. Born in 1960 in the city's Touro Hospital, Smith grew up in Metairie. A prolific collector of records, he had an avocational interest in music. He went to LSU and in 1983 received a degree in petroleum engineering. Five years working for Shell Oil had him wondering if maybe he should "try something else." He got an MBA from Loyola with the intention of working in the music business. After a few months booking road acts for a local music club, petroleum engineer/MBA Smith found himself at loose ends, eventually selling music at Record Ron's in the Quarter.

That's where he met Jerry Brock, a cofounder of WWOZ, who wanted to open an independent store specializing in New Orleans music. An intrigued Smith signed on as a partner, and the first LMF opened on St. Peters Street in 1992. From the beginning, in-store performances showcased local talent such as Snooks Eaglin, Danny Barker, and Tuba Fats. In 2001, Smith bought Brock out. LMF has gained a reputation as one of the country's best independent music stores, and Smith is considered a champion of the city's musical traditions.

Smith's LMF is an informal, old-style record store, the kind of spot where customers can browse comfortably for just the right CD or vinyl record. His highly personal office contains an unusual collection of signs from the thirties and forties, with hundreds of returnable soft-drink bottles shelved on the walls. It probably wouldn't have worked at Shell, but in the Louisiana Music Factory, it works just fine.

IRMA THOMAS

The Soul Queen of New Orleans, R&B singer Irma Thomas, has to check on some greens and red beans that she is cooking. No pretension, no attitude on the part of this warm and gracious woman, recently moved back into her New Orleans East home she and her husband and manager Emile Jackson rebuilt after Katrina's destruction.

Many other homes in the modest neighborhood await restoration. Thomas has rare determination, a mindset that led this high school dropout to graduate from college when she was nearly sixty. "East and the Ninth Ward are my home. This house is where I am comfortable. May not be a showcase but it's good enough for me."

Thomas always remembers singing, saying, "I started in church and just thought it was something everybody did. I just didn't think you could make a living at it." Moving to New Orleans as an infant, Thomas immediately soaked up the city's music. "When I was four," she claims, "I would go to Del P's, a bar on Clio and Loyola, and listen to the juke box. Momma always knew where to find me." Singing in her Baptist choir, she first recorded with Cosimo Matassa for her junior high school. Pregnant at fourteen, twice married by nineteen and with four children, she dropped out of school and worked as a waitress at the Pimlico Club on South Broad and Eve. She lost that job because "I was always singing," an unintentionally lucky break that led to the club's band leader, Tommy Ridgley, hiring her for her first paying gig and helping her to secure a record deal.

What followed for Thomas has been a brilliant, occasionally intermittent career during which she has recorded for legendary labels such as Minit, Chess, Atlantic, and Rounder and sung with the likes of B. B. King, James Brown, and Bonnie Raitt. The demands of motherhood and the climate of New Orleans interfered—after Hurricane Camille in 1969, Thomas moved to California, where she worked in a department store to support her family. By 1976, she was back in New Orleans, singing, "Nowhere else are there so many musicians who can make you sound so good." She's been at it ever since.

For years, Thomas did her cooking (and singing) at the Lion's Den, a Gravier Street club that she owned until it too was destroyed by Katrina. With a voice that David Torkanowsky has said "just drips with soul," Thomas still sings with her church choir. Her journey through the city's music is still firmly grounded in the same kind of scene in which she started back in 1947. Clearly, divas need not apply.

DAVID TORKANOWSKY

The Camp Street studio of David Torkanowsky is appropriate for someone who has a reputation as a bit of a Renaissance man. The dark, curly-haired "Tork" is an accomplished jazz pianist, composer, and producer. His studio reflects these talents with lots of instruments, plenty of recording equipment, and a comfortable couch for conversation. Seemingly friends with everyone in the city's music community, Torkanowsky knows how to tell a good story—for example, the one about the famously bizarre James Booker wearing a diaper held up with a gold safety pin and brandishing a pistol while playing piano at Tipitina's.

Torkanowsky's studio equipment includes two high-end microphones recently given to him by legendary New Orleans studio owner and engineer, Cosimo Matassa ("I wanted to give these to somebody who knows how to put them to good use"). Tork is paying the freight to restore the historical equipment, exclaiming, "Good Lord, how can I not? These are the same damn mikes that recorded 'Tutti Frutti' and 'The Fat Man.'"

With bloodlines unusual even by New Orleans standards, Tork is the son of German conductor Werner Torkanowsky, the musical director of the New Orleans Philharmonic-Symphony Orchestra from 1963 until 1977. His mother was a flamenco dancer who "entertained Gypsies while my father jammed with them on his violin." He grew up on Prytania Street in the city's Uptown area.

Torkanowsky began his musical career with jazz and classical piano lessons, for which he claimed to lack the self-discipline. He preferred to learn by listening to the village elders of New Orleans—Ellis Marsalis, Professor Longhair, Danny Barker, and the musicians of Preservation Hall; "That's how I became a piano player and not a pianist." A member of the progressive jazz group Astral Project from 1977 until 2000, Torkanowsky also is a composer and producer. He spent time in Hollywood writing for the TV series *Crime Stories* and managing the career of jazz singer Dianne Reeves.

"Tork" now lives in the Broadmoor neighborhood of New Orleans. Humorous and self-deprecating, he is a fixture in the city's music and social scene, playing with musicians such as Irvin Mayfield and Zachary Richard and hanging out with writer Harry Shearer and his friends. He remains surprised that he is a musician, claiming, "I am such an easily distracted under-achiever, I am amazed I can actually make a living doing this." He cherishes the city's "oral and aural traditions, its celebrations of the past that allows it to sustain music like no other place I have ever been."

ALLEN TOUSSAINT

Ask a New Orleans musician who in the city had the greatest impact on their craft and the answer you hear most often is Allen Toussaint, the regal R&B, jazz, and funk pianist, composer, arranger, and producer. Drive up to his 1950s-style home near Lake Pontchartrain and you know you're in the right place when you see the musical notes subtly displayed in his wrought-iron fence. Walk in to meet him and you are immediately struck by his impeccable manners and style, dressed in a suit and tie, the only musician of those interviewed that you naturally call "Mister" in deference to his dignity and presence.

At first, the quiet Toussaint, who is scheduled to leave for Europe soon after our meeting finishes, is reserved. He stands with perfect posture next to his pool table. Then, when his old friend Snooks Eaglin, the blind guitarist who died in 2009, is mentioned, Toussaint smiles and visibly relaxes. In 1952, the fourteen-year-old Toussaint recruited Eaglin for his R&B band, the Flamingos. When asked, Toussaint confirms as "absolutely true" the old story that the blind Eaglin once drove his inebriated bandmates home from a late-night gig, using the gravel shoulders to stay on the road.

Toussaint grew up in Gert Town, awash in the R&B scene that engulfed New Orleans in the 1940s and 1950s. Snooks, Huey Smith, Earl King, Fats Domino, Lloyd Price, Deacon John—so much talent surrounded Toussaint that he began producing, mostly for Minit Records. In the 1960s, he continued producing and writing for locals such as Irma Thomas, Ernie K-Doe, and Aaron Neville. Some of the most popular songs of the time were Toussaint's: "Working in the Coal Mine," "Mother-in-Law," and "Lipstick Traces," to name a few.

In the 1970s, Toussaint expanded his range into funk with continued success as a writer, singer, and composer. His gracious demeanor allows him to be a willing collaborator. He worked with Dr. John and the Meters and launched his own solo career, highlighted by the iconic *Southern Nights*. A collaboration with Patti Labelle led to the hit "Lady Marmalade," followed by "Yes We Can Can," sung by the Pointer Sisters and authored by Toussaint, who has made it his own post-Katrina anthem. The storm increased Toussaint's visibility, leading to his acclaimed collaboration with Elvis Costello, *The River in Reverse,* and *The Bright Mississippi*, his own interpretation of traditional New Orleans music.

Not long after his photo session, Toussaint was seen entering Galatoire's for a Friday-night dinner. In this bastion of the New Orleans establishment, everyone recognized that musical royalty was in the house. Waiters stepped aside and welcomed "Mr. Toussaint," guiding him to his table. Diners quietly noted his presence while respecting his privacy. Maybe Elton John said it best—meeting Allen Toussaint is like "meeting the Dalai Lama."

TROY TURNER

Riding his motorcycle, blues guitarist Troy Turner pulls up in front of J Monque'D's Uptown shotgun. He lives nearby in the Irish Channel. He is bringing food to J, who helped raise Turner in Baton Rouge and gave him his first paying gig at fourteen. The precise nature of their relationship as described by J is a little unclear ("I was sweet on Troy's grandmother"), but it is evident that the two are very close, sharing music, the blues, and some of the same demons.

Turner relaxes on J Monque'D's front porch, listening and laughing at the harmonica player's many stories. He values J's prolific advice: "He's the one who told me never let the audience be better dressed than you are. And if at all possible, avoid playing 'Mustang Sally.' You'll get so many requests for it during your career, it can drive you crazy."

Turner comes by his hardscrabble background honestly, claiming to be the nephew of soul singer Ike Turner, who had his own issues. There was plenty of pain in Turner's early Baton Rouge childhood, with too much poverty and too many abusive relationships. He needed J to help him through it, along with music, first gospel and then guitar. He made his way to New Orleans and played one of his first gigs at the Maple Leaf Bar. Success came fast to Turner, who in his early twenties gained a reputation as one of the city's hottest blues guitarists, compared to Stevie Ray Vaughan and B. B. King. He recorded with Derek Trucks and the Allman Brothers. But it proved more than Turner could handle—"I got too much too early, had a big ego, was driving a Mercedes way before I deserved to." Drugs and prison were the result.

But Turner got past that following a successful rehab. After a ten-year recording hiatus, he released a generally well-received blues album in 2010. He played Jazz Fest in 2011, again after being absent from that stage for more than a decade. His style has evolved to encompass some funk, some soul, and some rock. A self-described "Bourbon Street itinerant," he regularly plays gigs all over the Quarter.

Katrina was tough on Turner, who lost everything and slept for a while in a homeless shelter on Esplanade (but à la J's admonition, always wore a suit for his Bourbon Street performances). He openly acknowledges that, in some ways, his life has been a bluesman's cliché. Cliché or not, the gentle Turner is now comfortable where he is, the kind of workaday musician who is an essential part of the city's musical fabric.

DON VAPPIE

Valence Street in Uptown New Orleans has been home to plenty of the city's great musicians—a bunch of Nevilles, jazz trumpeter Teddy Riley, harmonica player J Monque'D. Jazz banjo player Don Vappie lived on Valence for a few years after his birth. It was no surprise that he would return to a street so rich in musical heritage when he picked the place for his photograph.

Vappie is Creole through and through, capturing the creativity and contradictions of that complex culture. He loves the easy familiarity of the city's streets. He wasn't really aware of any racial divisions until he helped integrate De La Salle High School in the late 1960s. Even then, music and places such as Preservation Hall transcended barriers of black and white.

Vappie comes by his musical talents honestly. He is related to early jazz great, Papa John Joseph, who, as Vappie tells the story, stood up after a particularly rousing Preservation Hall rendition of "When the Saints Go Marching In," and said, "That one about did me in." Sadly, he was right, collapsing and dying right there. Vappie first played bass in the 1970s funk band, Trac One. Inspired by Danny Barker, he soon developed a passion for the city's jazz traditions and the six-string and tenor banjos. Scorned by some in the black community for its minstrel show symbolism, the banjo actually has a rich African heritage, which Vappie understands: "The banjo is part of our street rhythms, blending African, Caribbean, and American sounds, making us who we are."

Vappie started the Creole Jazz Serenaders and became a leading interpreter of traditional musicians such as Jelly Roll Morton and King Oliver. After Katrina, he wasn't sure he wanted to return to the city, concerned it would be too tough to earn a living. His wife, Millie, knew better, no matter what jobs proved to be available, because her husband needed New Orleans as much as New Orleans needed him. When they returned, they did so with charitable vengeance, starting the Bring It On Home organization to help musicians get paying gigs after the storm.

Vappie is stubborn and opinionated, occasionally cantankerous, and always proud of his Creole heritage. To Vappie, that term defies simple characterization but provides ample explanation of what New Orleans is. As he said in the documentary *American Creole: New Orleans Reunion,* "What I call Creole are New Orleans people who aren't white and aren't black. We're a mix of French, Spanish, African, and American Indian, and that mixture made this city what it is." And that mixture also helped to make Don Vappie what he is: the finest jazz-banjo player in the world.

JOHNNY VIDACOVICH

Walking into the Mid-City home of Johnny Vidacovich, we are not surprised to find the animated drummer giving a lesson to a young Canadian who has just arrived in the city to learn from Vidacovich and the city's other legendary percussionists. In an accent re-affirming that New Orleans really can sound like Brooklyn, Vidacovich imparts his almost Yoda-like philosophy of drumming: "Keep your pants unbuttoned to remember to breathe. Don't hang around with just drummers; hang out with other musicians to become a drummer. Take in the externals for a few years, but if you really want to drum, it has to be about your own internals. As you age, shed, simplify, [and] work the breaks. What you don't play is as important as what you do."

Vidacovich loves teaching in his living room. His students have included Stanton Moore, Brian Blade, and plenty of others. It is an unpretentious setting with at least four dogs, several sets of drums, and Vidacovich's family members wandering in and out.

Born and raised in Mid-City, Vidacovich began drumming when he was only ten and fascinated with R&B. By seventeen, he was playing in Bourbon Street strip clubs, where he learned his minimalist style, explaining, "Can't be over-playing for strippers, it's their show." Within a few years, he was performing with Professor Longhair, Mose Allison, and James Booker. An original member of the Astral Project, one of the city's preeminent modern jazz groups, Vidacovich blends the traditional and the innovative and is a skilled master improviser. He has appeared in more than 250 recordings and gigs all over the world.

With his open personality and gregarious style, Vidacovich is a popular member of the city's musical community. After his house suffered damage from Hurricane Katrina, former student Stanton Moore launched a successful Internet campaign to help fund repairs. Vidacovich was deeply appreciative, grateful to be part of a special family he once described in a memorable interview with *Offbeat* magazine: "There's so many musicians around here. I don't mean popular, fancy, well-known, rich ones—I mean natural musicians. Children being born, children coming up—it's morphic resonance. It's in the air."

And he means that literally. Vidacovich claims to have figured out what makes his hometown special. "We are below sea level." He continues, "Molecules are thicker down here. Drumming is harder in the heavy air. So when you go anywhere else, it's a lot easier. We're isolated; it's not easy to get out through all that water, but that's what makes our music." Given the results, it makes sense to us.

WASHBOARD CHAZ

ven though he only arrived in New Orleans in 2000, washboard player Washboard Chaz Leary is a fixture on Frenchmen Street, the city's musical epicenter. Relaxed and unassuming, he has his morning coffee in a café next to Snug Harbor and across the street from the Spotted Cat, where he has had a regular gig for years.

The trim Leary looks like a professor. But when he speaks, it is evident that he is all about his music. During his time in the city, the affable percussionist has earned a reputation as someone whose friendly personality allows him to play with practically any of the city's musicians. Post-storm, Leary thinks the musical community has grown even friendlier, with "very few cliques, an infusion of good young talent." Leary will play it all, from blues to jazz to western swing and is willing to change genres depending on who is taking the lead.

A native New Yorker, Leary got early rhythm playing in a drum and bugle corps. He was intrigued by percussion, by the be-bop sounds of Roy Haynes and Max Roach. He has played the washboard for more than forty years. After living in Colorado for a couple of decades, he moved to New Orleans at the turn of the millennium, in part to rediscover his percussionist, be-bop roots. He played some on Jackson Square, especially with Tuba Fats, and,

relying on friends he had in town, he eventually formed the Washboard Chaz Blues Trio.

Unlike other washboard players, Leary does not play with a drummer. Using his board's wood frame and a hotel call bell, he provides his own drum-like percussion. He uses thimbles—lots of them—and recently placed an order for four hundred in all sizes. His energy is inexhaustible, his bands numerous: the Trio, the Washboard Rodeo, the Palmetto Bug Stompers, the Valparaiso Men's Chorus, the Mirlitones, and the Tin Men, which he formed with guitarist Alex McMurray and sousaphonist Matt Perrine. He matches styles as needed, from Helen Gillet to John Rankin to Supagroup.

Given Leary's energy and popularity, it was only a matter of time before a festival would take his name. ChazFest was created in 2006 after the Tin Men did not receive an invitation to play the first Jazz Fest after Hurricane Katrina. Leary, McMurray, and Perrine decided to host a festival for uninvited musicians. Hence ChazFest, a one day Bywater festival now held every year between Jazz Fest weekends. A modest Leary claims it is only named after him because "jazz rhymes with Chaz, otherwise it is Alex Fest." Perhaps, but as the only musician to play every year with every act that performs, Washboard certainly can lay fair claim to his own ChazFest.

BIG SAM WILLIAMS

The hip bar of a downtown boutique hotel may seem like an unusual spot for a hard-partying trombonist like Big Sam Williams to choose for his photograph, but not if you appreciate the vibe of the Loa Bar and the history of the International House Hotel. Both pay homage to the city's past while looking ahead to its creative future. Much the same could be said of Big Sam.

The 100-plus-year-old hotel is in a Beaux Arts building, which, for its first eighty-five years, housed a bank and then a trade center. It became a hotel in 1998, proclaimed on its website as "a sophisticated sanctuary, a mecca of sorts for the forward-looking artisans, entrepreneurs, and visitors who are reinventing the great city of New Orleans." The bar is named for the voodoo spirits who intercede on behalf of humans with the benevolent voodoo god. It is a natural choice for Big Sam, great-grandson of the legendary and mystical Buddy Bolden, himself the architect of a new sound that blends deep New Orleans brass with a distinctive funk and polished R&B groove.

From growing up Uptown in the Twelfth Ward near Tipitina's, the urbane Williams later lived in Gentilly and New Orleans East. He was taught by Kid Jordan, marched in school bands, and attended the New Orleans Center for Creative Arts. It was around then when he first heard the Dirty Dozen Brass Band. Not long after, Williams attended a sweet-sixteen birthday party for a NOCCA classmate, where he realized her father was Dirty Dozen trumpet player Efrem Towns. After a three-hour conversation with Towns, Sam volunteered that if the Dozen ever needed another trombonist, he was "available." Several months later, Towns called to see if Sam was indeed available. He was, and they left the next day for a two-month tour.

Williams played with the Dirty Dozen for the next four years, mixing touring with classes at the University of New Orleans and with his own band, Funky Nation, which he started in 2002. Williams left the Dirty Dozen, to whom he remains close ("once a Dozen, always a Dozen"), in order to concentrate his efforts on Funky Nation. He soon had a regular gig at the Funky Butt club, whose owner, Shanekah Peterson, he married in 2006. His vibrant performances at Jazz Fest and Voodoo Fest and especially in local clubs, where his exuberant style makes him "all about the party," are legendary. He plays all over town "with anybody, different cats every night, no pigeonholes in music here."

Big Sam is in great shape. He had just played a rousing set at Voodoo Fest. The night before his picture, he had watched a Saints Sunday-night football game and then played at Tipitina's until 4:30 A.M. After the shoot, he was going to the gym to work out. A bar named after benevolent voodoo spirits was a good place for a short respite from a busy schedule.

AFTERWORD

Our sincere hope is that you have enjoyed *When Not Performing*. We also hope that you realize and appreciate how we tried to provide you with a window through which you can see and learn something about the large and ever-changing musical community of New Orleans. By design, the book wasn't divided into genres—that would be too limiting. A musician in this city must be able to easily cross over into different styles. Flexibility is the name of the game. A common occurrence is having a traditional jazz player sit in with a blues or funk band or vice versa. Even in clubs and private parties, the audiences want and demand a large variety of music. As one of the musicians affirmed, it is our job to give them what they want, and it better be good. In the musical world, you are only as good as your last performance.

Many thanks to the musicians who made this a wonderfully fun project. They are truly one of our greatest assets, adding to and inspiring the magic of New Orleanian food, architecture, and people. They are accessible, brilliant, and extremely eccentric. How can you not love them all?

From the outset, we knew that we couldn't cover everything. The desire was to give a good sampling, touching on different styles and proving that there is something for everyone. Perhaps there will be some hurt feelings; many may wonder why they weren't included. Let us reassure you—it was not deliberate! Limited time and space, difficult schedules, and the challenge of locating performers all contributed to narrowing the field of subjects.

Fortunately, Pelican Publishing wanted to bring this project to fruition. Born and bred here, they understood and appreciated the idea at the outset. The team there has added an old-world work ethic and craftsmanship to this book, which makes us proud. From the very beginning, we've been surrounded by a group of people whose only goal was to produce the very best book possible.

Louis Armstrong may have said it best: when asked about his music, he said, "My whole life, my whole soul, my whole spirit is to blow that horn." Our hope is that you can see and feel that in these pictures and words. His legacy is alive and well here in New Orleans.

More later,

David G. Spielman
Fred Lyon
New Orleans

160